The Basics: I

Christianity

Peter Pawlowsky

SCM PRESS LTD
Trinity Press International

Translated by John Bowden from the German *Christentum,*
published 1994 by hpt-Verlagsgesellschaft m.b.H & Co. KG,
Vienna, in the series *kurz und bündig*, edited by Wolf In der Maur.

Library of Congress Cataloging-in-Publication Data
Pawlowsky, Peter.
    [Christentum. English]
    Christianity / Peter Pawlowsky. — 1st US ed.
        p.   cm.
    Includes bibliographical references.
    ISBN 1-56338-112-5 :
    1. Church history. 2. Christianity I. Title.
BR150.P38   1995
270—dc20   94-47513

First U.S. edition
published 1995 by Trinity Press International
P.O. Box 1321, Harrisburg, PA 17105
Trinity Press International is a division of the Morehouse Group.
First British edition published 1995
by SCM Press Ltd.

Typeset at the Spartan Press Ltd,
Lymington, Hants

Printed in the United States of America
98 99 00 01 02 03 04 05 8 7 6 5 4 3 2

Contents

Chronological table

1096	First Crusade to the Holy Land followed by six more up to 1270.
1123	First to Fourth Lateran Councils within a century, ending in 1215
1184	Peter Waldo and his followers are excommunicated
1209	Francis of Assisi becomes an itinerant preacher
1209–29	Albigensian wars in Southern France against the Cathars and Waldensians
1232	Establishment of the papal Inquisition
1245	First Council of Lyons
1274	Second Council of Lyons; Thomas Aquinas dies
1311–12	Council of Vienne
1414–18	Council of Constance; burning of Jan Hus (1415)
1438–45	Council of Basel/Ferrara/Florence
1493	Byzantium is captured by the Muslim Ottomans
1512–17	Fifth Lateran Council
1517	Martin Luther publishes his 95 Theses against indulgences. Beginning of the Reformation
from 1523	Reformation in Zurich (Ulrich Zwingli)
from 1526	Reformation in Northern Europe
1530	Protestant Augsburg Confession
1534	Separation of the Anglican Church from Rome
from 1536	Reformation in Geneva (Jean Calvin)
1545–63	Council of Trent
from 1558	Counter-Reformation in Bavaria
1562–98	Huguenot wars in France
1566	Protestant Second (final) Helvetic Confession
1589	Orthodox Patriarchate in Moscow
1598/1621	Beginning of the Counter-Reformation in the Habsburg countries

1595–96   Brest-Litovsk Union of the White Russians and Ukrainians with Rome. A model for the later Catholic Eastern churches

1609   First Baptist community in Amsterdam

1618–48   Thirty Years' War in Germany

1620   Battle of the White Mountain: defeat of the Bohemian Protestants

1620   The Pilgrim Fathers emigrate to America

1653   The Old Believers split off from Russian Orthodoxy

1738   Beginning of Methodism

1781   Emperor Joseph II's Edict of Tolerance

1789   French Revolution. Declaration on Human Rights, including freedom of religion

from 1830 Origin of independent Orthodox churches and patriarchates in the new nation states of Eastern Europe

1869–70   First Vatican Council

1870   End of the Papal States

1871/1875 Foundation of the Old Catholic Church/Union of Utrecht

1878   International Missionary Conference in London

1900   World Missionary Conference in New York

1905   Separation of church and state in France

1910   World Missionary Conference in Edinburgh

1947   Foundation of the Lutheran World Federation (forerunners since 1923)

1948ff.   Foundation of the World Council of Churches in Amsterdam; further assemblies to the present day in Evanston, New Delhi, Uppsala, Nairobi, Vancouver and Canberra

1962–65   Second Vatican Council

1970   Foundation of the Reformed World Alliance (forerunners since 1875)

Palestine in the Year Zero

**Christianity has its roots in Judaism; it began as a
Jewish sect and for centuries attempted to suppress the
memory of this origin by persecuting and condemning
Jews. Jesus and all his contemporary followers were
Jews and had deep roots in the Jewish tradition. So
investigations into the religion of Christians must
begin in the Near East.**

Anatomy of a witches' cauldron

To talk of Palestine at the beginning of our era is to
anticipate the Christian interpretation of history. Was the
time in which Jesus of Nazareth was born in fact a turning
point? There are some indications of that. With the
deposition of the last ruler of the Maccabaean dynasty in 37
BCE, an epoch came to an end. 130 years earlier (in 167
BCE), through a successful rebellion, the Maccabees had
won the last century of political independence (before the
foundation of the state of Israel in 1948) for the Jewish
people. The successor of the last of the Maccabees was
Herod the Great – as a Jew still master in his own land, but
nominated by the Romans and dependent on co-operation
with them to sustain the unstable political balance in the
Near East.

Herod was attracted by the open culture of Hellenism; he
saw himself as a cosmopolitan, was a friend of the emperor
Augustus and had ten wives of different religions and
nationalities. Thus to what we would now call orthodox
Jews he was a traitor to the cause for which the Maccabees

had fought. At the same time Herod gave these orthodox Jews a new symbol and focal point: he began to rebuild the Jerusalem temple in splendour; its foundation, the Wailing Wall, is still the most sacred place in Judaism.

Herod built not only the temple but also palaces and fortresses, including the fortified city of Masada by the Dead Sea. This was to become the symbol of the last Jewish resistance against the Romans after the final fall of Jerusalem (in 70 CE). This enormous building activity was not just the expression of a royal desire for pomp, but also a solid programme to provide employment. When he began rebuilding the temple (in 20 BCE), Herod employed 11,000 workers in Jerusalem – at that time a city of 25,000 inhabitants. And when the building work was halted, long after his death, between 62 and 64 CE, the authorities were faced with the problem of how to cope with the unemployment of the 18,000 who had been laid off. The presence of a host of men who had been socially uprooted made conditions unstable. Palestine was overpopulated for the circumstances of the time, and Jewish merchants and craftsmen looked for new openings throughout the Mediterranean area. Penniless farmers and agricultural workers who could not go abroad formed an explosive proletariat; not only had Herod employed them in his building programme, but he and his successors attempted to bond them together by founding numerous cities (e.g. Caesarea and Tiberias) and resettling them.

However, Herod's ambition also intensified the very evil that he was fighting against. The building work cost enormous sums. So the tax screw was increasingly tightened and drove the common people either into slavery for debt or towards robber bands and revolutionary groups which gathered in the areas on the edge of the wildernesses. In Palestine at that time three taxes were levied: by the king, by the temple hierarchy and by the Romans. Herod confiscated the land of farmers who were unable to pay and created estates which grew larger and larger; these often came into the possession of great Roman landowners, for whom only export produce counted. The situation had parallels with present-day Latin America: a few people who were getting richer and richer controlled the land, and the mass of the poor were exposed to their every whim and went hungry. In addition there were catastrophes (drought, epidemics and earthquakes at the beginning of the first century), and supply difficulties throughout the Roman empire led to a great famine in Palestine in the years 46 and 47 CE.

Prophets and terrorists

Such times nurture apocalyptic anxieties and revolutionary ideas. Herod himself had managed to hold down the growing tensions, but after he died in 4 BCE all kinds of aggression and disillusionment were let loose. A rebellion – one of the many which were to occur in the next decades – broke out in Galilee, led by a certain Judas. Various prophets promised miracles as a sign of imminent political change. Agitations of this kind were always suspect to the Romans, and often they put an end to the activities of such gurus and their followers with a bloodbath, as a deterrent. If naive idealists often got caught up in such cleansing actions, the Romans were well aware that armed rebellion could be sparked off by any revolt.

In 6 CE the Syrian governor Quirinius put Judaea under direct Roman administration, which amounted to a definitive annexation, and ordered a census in order to organize the collection of taxes. That was the signal for Judas and a Pharisee named Zadok: they combined various underground organizations to form the Zealot party. They proclaimed the 'sole rule of God', and called for the violent expulsion of the Roman occupying forces and the deposition of the local kings who collaborated with the Romans. The Zealots had nothing to lose and therefore took no heed of anything or anyone. They organized terrorist attacks and made even Jerusalem unsafe: Sicarii (dagger men) murdered indiscriminately among the pilgrim throngs, where they could immediately merge into the crowd.

Jerusalem and the temple were dominated by the priestly aristocracy of the Sadducees, who lived mainly on the pilgrimage tourism. In addition, every Jew had to pay them a tithe and a temple tax. The Sadducees adopted a dual strategy: they collaborated with the Romans because any disruption to public order endangered pilgrimages, their economic basis; but at the same time they made it clear to the people that the Roman occupying forces were to blame for anything that caused discontent in the land. So the Sadducees attempted to safeguard their very limited local power, shielded from the increasing aggressiveness.

Both the Zealots and the Jerusalem elite had party programmes backed by religious arguments; but questions of power were clearly in the foreground. Two other groups expected a change from what would really be a religious renewal: these were the Essenes and the Pharisees. The Essenes with their central monastic settlement of Qumran by the Dead Sea attempted to prepare for the rule of God by following the biblical commandments about purity with radical strictness. They built up an enclosed, pure 'alternative society', and although they were regarded as being peaceful, in their fantasies about what would happen when God took power in the future they pictured a bloody orgy in which all apostates and aliens would perish. The core group of Essenes lived a celibate life without private possessions.

The Pharisees similarly saw salvation in a stricter observance of the Law, i.e. the Torah (the biblical instructions as laid down in the five books of Moses). However, their concern was not withdrawal and separation; rather, they wanted to renew the normal everyday life of Jewish society. For that, it was necessary not only to insist on faithfulness to the Law but also to adapt the Law pragmatically to everyday situations – a dilemma which the Pharisees were not always able to resolve and which sometimes brought them the reputation of being hypocrites or masters of legal pedantry. Nevertheless, Pharisaism was the only realistic renewal movement and – as was to transpire – the only one with a future. The Pharisees, who were for the most part laymen, put study of the biblical law, the Torah, on the same level as the priestly temple cult which hitherto had indisputably had the highest religious status. They disputed among themselves as to which was more important, rigorous faithfulness to the law – thus the school of Rabbi Shammai – or a faithfulness to the law which took practical questions of everyday life into account – thus the school of Rabbi Hillel. The more liberal Hillel school prevailed, and rescued Judaism after the downfall of Jerusalem and the destruction of the temple.

In addition there were also Hellenistic Jews living in Palestine, who had returned from the Diaspora and were drawn to the international culture of the Mediterranean area at that time. The strict believers native to the land were never able to establish friendly relations with them, a conflict which was still to be potentially explosive in the early days of Christianity.

No precise knowledge about Jesus

In this religious and political witches' cauldron, in a society which was becoming increasingly unstable, around the year 30 CE a man appeared who called himself Jesus. He came from Nazareth in Galilee, that district in the north which could always be counted on to cause unrest; around three years later he was executed. Jesus was one of the itinerant preachers and prophets who at that time kept causing a temporary stir in the land. The Romans gave them short shrift. Jesus himself did not leave anything in writing, and only a few passages outside the Bible refer to him in passing. The historians of the time had no more than subordinate clauses for Jesus; the events taking place around him did not suggest that he had any greater historical significance.

The texts of the New Testament were written down some decades after the events and contain very few historical references. So the date of Jesus' birth is on the one hand put back into the reign of Herod, who died in the year 4 before our reckoning, and on the other connected with the census made by the Syrian governor Quirinius, who did not take office until ten years later.

The conjectures about the actual year in which Jesus was born fluctuate between 12 and 2 BCE. We have rather more precise information about the period of Jesus' public ministry. He seems first to have lived in the group formed by another preacher, the John who preached by the Jordan and baptized. John was executed in 29 CE. Around a year later, at any rate in the period when the Roman procurator Pontius Pilate held office (27–36 CE), Jesus was crucified.

Hope for the Messiah is still the future perspective of Jewish faith and was particularly prevalent at the time of Jesus. Jesus of Nazareth was not the only one to be regarded as Messiah at that time.

Historically speaking, the central figure of Christianity in no way towers above the events of his time; so how could a world religion nevertheless develop in connection with the man from Nazareth?

2

History in Sermons

The Jewish Bible is also a holy book for Christians; however, they call it 'Old Testament', since they have supplemented it with their own writings, the 'New Testament'. In it Jesus is proclaimed as the one sent by God at the turning point of the ages.

The New Testament

In complete contrast to the sparse data in non-Christian historians, Jesus of Nazareth is the central person in a whole series of writings. The canon of Christian texts was formed from the many texts handed down as the church made up its mind about them between the second and the fourth century. It comprises twenty-seven works in all, which were written in the period between 51/52 and 120 to 130. We know little about the authors. Seven letters certainly come from Paul: the letter to the Romans, the two letters to the Corinthians, the letters to the Galatians and the Philippians, the first letter to the Thessalonians and the letter to Philemon. Paul's authorship of the letters to the Ephesians and the Colossians is disputed; the other so-called Pauline letters certainly do not come from him, but were only composed after his death and attributed to him. Luke with his Gospel and Acts is another tangible figure, but of the other authors we have only the names or, similarly, attributions after the death of the alleged authors.

The New Testament writings contain information which is historically quite reliable, but their interest is not in

The New Testament

The twenty-seven books	Date of composition	Abbreviation
Gospel according to Matthew	80–90	Matt.
Gospel according to Mark	65–70	Mark
Gospel according to Luke	80–90	Luke
Gospel according to John	90–100	John
Acts of the Apostles	shortly after Luke	Acts
Letter to the Romans	58	Rom.
First Letter to the Corinthians	c.57	I Cor.
Second Letter to the Corinthians	shortly after I Cor.	II Cor.
Letter to the Galatians	54–56	Gal.
Letter to the Ephesians	80–90	Eph.
Letter to the Philippians	61–63	Phil.
Letter to the Colossians	? post-Pauline	Col.
First Letter to the Thessalonians	50–51	I Thess.
Second Letter to the Thessalonians	shortly after II Thess.	I Thess.
First Letter to Timothy	c.100	I Tim.
Second Letter to Timothy	c.100	II Tim.
Letter to Titus	c.100	Titus
Letter to Philemon	63	Philemon
Letter to the Hebrews	90–100	Heb.
Letter of James	90–100	James
First Letter of Peter	80–100	I Peter
Second Letter of Peter	120–130	II Peter
First Letter of John	c.100	John
Second Letter of John	c.100	I John
Third Letter of John	c.100	III John
Letter of Jude	c.100	Jude
Revelation of John	80–100	Rev.

historiography. Rather, even where they are reporting events, they put them in the context of their interest – namely of retelling their experience with Jesus of Nazareth. They seek to convey a conviction, they preach – that is why the authors composed these works; that is why they select or omit and put events in new contexts.

The question of the origin of Christianity is difficult to answer because it is already present in the earliest writings: after the death of Jesus at first only a disappointed group of followers was left behind, thinking of anything but founding a new religion. More than twenty dark years lie between the crucifixion and the earliest text of the New Testament, the First Letter of Paul to the Thessalonians. During these years a revaluation of the life and death of Jesus took place; a new view of the salvation history of the Bible was developed; and the first steps were taken towards separation from the mother religion, Judaism.

A Jewish sect

As early as around the year 33 (according to other calculations three years later) a certain Stephen may have confessed his belief in Jesus as Christ and Messiah so clearly in Jerusalem that he was stoned for it. This was an act of lynch law, and people's emotions were probably directed against Stephen not only as a Christian but also as a Hellenistic Jew who was not a member of one of the local nationalistic religious cliques; even the conservative Jewish Christians had their difficulties with such brethren in the faith. Shortly afterwards, between 34 and 37, the Pharisee Saul, who according to the account in the Acts of the Apostles had a hand in the stoning of Stephen, changed sides and joined the new sect of the followers of Jesus: Saul became a Paul. Already at the beginning of the 40s both Paul and Peter, at that time head of the earliest community in Jerusalem, embarked on the first missionary journeys. The sect of the followers of Jesus began to make a mark. The famine of 46/ 47 also caused difficulties for the earliest community in Jerusalem, but there had already long been communities outside the heartlands of Judaism, and in them money was collected for Jerusalem – for example in Antioch, where the designation 'Christians' first appears. Peter left Jerusalem; his successor as head of the community was James, called 'brother of the Lord' (i.e. the Lord Jesus). He attempted to mediate between conservative and Hellenistic liberal Jewish Christians and between Jewish and Gentile Christians. But he suffered the same fate as Stephen: he was martyred around 62.

By this time the first letters of Paul, which were later to be counted among the earliest parts of the New Testament, had already been in circulation for a decade. That means that after twenty years the most important characteristics of Christianity were fixed. Evidently the very first three to five years of this period were sufficient time for the power of the new faith to become so established that the first martyrs were giving their lives for it. It was during the years, perhaps only months, immediately after the death of Jesus that the disappointed sect of a little-heeded Jewish itinerant preacher mutated into a potential world religion.

What Jesus really said

In order to understand the dynamics of these years we need to know what Jesus himself preached and how his followers understood this preaching after his death. For one thing is certain: the followers of Jesus saw their teacher as more than a prophet. They called him the Christ, which is a straight Greek translation of the Hebrew 'Messiah', i.e. the anointed, the saving king of the end-time. By contrast, there are many texts in the Gospels in which Jesus in no way proclaims himself as Messiah but promises the imminent beginning of the kingdom of God, i.e. the end time. In such passages we are nearer to the 'original text' of Jesus than where a solemn theological retrospect has crept in. Thus the preaching *of* Jesus can be distinguished from the preaching after and *about* Jesus.

Jesus preached the kingdom of God as an event which would break in within the shortest possible time. With the kingdom of God was associated the notion of an end to history and a completion and new creation of the world and human beings; the kingdom was to bring a transformation of all values and an end to hatred, injustice, mourning and death; an end to finitude generally and thus also to 'sin', a term which in the Bible denotes the human 'proneness towards evil'.

Jesus did not side either with the Zealots, because the kingdom of God cannot be brought in by force, or with the Essenes, who had withdrawn into their monastic alternative world. He was a charismatic preacher and healer who acted with the assurance of one who had been given full authority by God, and without doubt was already regarded by some as Messiah during his lifetime; however, in so far as messiahship meant bringing political liberation from the Roman occupying forces, Jesus distanced himself from it.

Along with his followers, Jesus led the life of an itinerant preacher, with no fixed abode, no family, no possessions, convinced that the world as it is would soon pass away. He was not a political or a social revolutionary, but perplexed people by not avoiding either the establishment or outsiders, by living with the poor but not fomenting war against the rich. Certainly he regarded riches as a serious obstacle, but he did not believe that the kingdom of God could be forced in through asceticism and penitential practices. So even his utterly simple life, without needs, could not protect him from being called a 'glutton and a drunkard' by his contemporaries, who made themselves out to be particularly pious.

His was a position between every possible stool. Even now its influence seems to derive from the fact that it brings liberation from prejudices and ideological fixations, and escapes being taken over by any side. However, that does not in itself explain how Jesus was more to his followers than one of the great sages of world history. It was his early and violent death and the conviction of his resurrection that gave his cause its decisive turning point.

The Beatitudes in the Sermon on the Mount are a hymn to the transformation of all current values in the end time:

'Blessed are the poor in spirit, for theirs is the kingdom of heaven.

Blessed are those who mourn, for they shall be comforted.

Blessed are the meek, for they shall inherit the earth.

Blessed are those who hunger and thirst for righteousness, for they shall be satisfied.

Blessed are the merciful, for they shall obtain mercy.

Blessed are the pure in heart, for they shall see God.

Blessed are the peacemakers, for they shall be called sons of God.

Blessed are those who are persecuted for righteousness' sake, for theirs is the kingdom of heaven.'

Gospel according to Matthew, Chapter 5

Death and resurrection

It is hard to see why a Galilean preacher should have gone to the cultic metropolis of Jerusalem, especially as Jesus seems to have behaved in anything but a diplomatic way. His anger at the unholy conditions there – far more tourism than pilgrimage – made him seem politically more danger-ous than he was. Thus tradition has it that Jesus drove the money-changers and those who sold animals for sacrifice from the temple because they were degrading the house of God into a market hall (John 2). After such a scene the Sadducees took steps to see that the peace would not be disturbed and came to an understanding with Pontius Pilate, who preferred to remove one potential troublemaker too many rather than one too few. For the followers of Jesus, that was the collapse of their dream that the end of the times had come and that they would be included among the leaders in the kingdom of God. Much as the messianic hope was current at this time, someone who had been crucified seemed to be disqualified from this dignity.

However, despair, disappointment and bitterness evi-dently could not completely quench what they had experi-enced over a number of years with Jesus, the confidence they had had in him, the degree to which they had believed his words. So which was real: yesterday's faith or today's disappointment? The answer to this question was the hour in which Christianity was born.

Certainly the sources omit a good deal here, since they are more interested in the event than in the process. If we take the narrative approach of the Bible seriously, it is possible to understand this process. Internal and external processes are reported as events because only their reality content counts; the question of historical facts is only raised from a narrower modern perspective. So an attempt at reconstruc-tion could look like this.

- After the crucifixion the disappointed and anxious followers of Jesus were primarily concerned not so much with the message of Jesus as with Jesus himself: in view of his fate was he still credible, or had belief in him been quenched by death?

- Faith in Jesus thus became the condition for the coming kingdom of God; the person of Jesus could no longer be separated from his message. Because his followers became aware that faith in their teacher was stronger than his death, there was no longer any doubt that the kingdom of God had already begun with Jesus himself.

- In this way the new, 'post-Easter', i.e. Christian faith, took shape for them: they now saw Jesus as the first human being in the perfected creation, the 'sinless one', over whom the tendency towards evil and death no longer had any power. The Jesus of history had become the Christ of faith.

- This view of things turned everything upside down. A Jesus who had been raised from the dead appeared to them, so that they had no doubt that he was alive and understood that he had not returned to his former life, but lived in the new mode of the kingdom of God, in which there is no longer any death (this is what Christians celebrate at Easter). The Gospels relate this in paradoxical imagery and scenes: he comes and disappears; he goes through closed doors, but also eats with his friends and allows himself to be touched before finally withdrawing from them (this is what Christians celebrate as Christ's ascension).

- These revolutionary experiences provoked enthusiasm in the literal sense: the Acts of the Apostles (in chapter 2) reports an intoxicating event which it calls the outpouring of the Holy Spirit and describes it in terms of the disappearance of all anxiety and an ability to speak in all languages (this is what Christians celebrate at Pentecost).

However we may attempt to think ourselves into this process of recognition, at all events from then on this Jesus acknowledged as Christ has exercised a new fascination: all available notions are measured by him and related to him. Many passages in the Jewish Bible appear all at once as prophetic forecasts of the death and resurrection of the new man, and are understood as 'scriptural proofs'. The conviction prevails that the resurrection was only the first step and that Jesus will soon return, finally to establish the kingdom of God which has been announced.

Jesus has time and again been understood as the great ethical model: as one who is committed on behalf of the poor and those without rights, as the one who plays off love against the law, as the first 'new man' in partnership with women, as a social revolutionary and martyr. All this may have been the case, but we would know no more about Jesus than about the other great figures of history had not the revaluation of his life taken place in the faith of his followers, who understood him as Messiah and Son of Man. That is the special and irreplaceable feature of the new religion.

3

What is 'Christology'?

Who was this Jesus Christ? This difficult question has occupied Christian theology right from the beginning. Already in the New Testament there are several different reflections on how the human and the divine can be thought of together in the central figure of Christianity.

Models for thought

One of the reflections starts with the baptism of Jesus by John in the Jordan. At that time, according to the biblical account in Mark (1.9–11), a voice from heaven said, 'You are my beloved Son!' This theological scheme implies that God accepted the man Jesus as his son ('adoptionist christology').

The Gospel according to John develops another perspective: Christ is the Logos, the creative word which already lived with the Father God before all time, which has now come into the world and is returning to the Father ('preexistence christology').

Whereas Paul is not interested in the theme of the virgin birth (it does not occur anywhere in his writings), it plays an important role in the stories of Jesus' infancy in Matthew and Luke: because according to the conviction of the evangelists Jesus is at the same time man and God, Mary conceived him from God himself ('Son of God christology').

In the course of history these earliest thought models were followed by many more, and have occupied theologians, bishops, popes and councils down to the present day. It is characteristic of Christian theology that it thinks in terms of contradictions which are held together yet kept apart. The fact that for centuries Europe was preoccupied with such dialectical forms of thought has not failed to have an influence on its culture, civilization and progress.

Regardless of what is thought of the belief, the event which tradition calls the 'incarnation' of God lies at the heart of Christianity and distinguishes this religion from all others. Christians are convinced that in the historical person Jesus of Nazareth God himself has become man, has experienced a human life from birth to death, and in this way has overcome what human beings cannot overcome: finitude, guilt and death. That brings about a radical change in the image of God. God is no longer the one who intervenes from outside, the Lord of history, but also the God who shows solidarity, who stands by human beings and shares their fate. God is not only the one in power but also the companion; the brother God stands alongside the creator and father God. All religions have an idea of God which recognizes the power and greatness of an other-worldly being transcending any human measure; Christianity shares this idea, but sets its opposite alongside it: God is not only timeless and almighty, but also gives himself over to human helplessness and history; God is to be found not only in an inaccessible beyond, not only in splendour and glory, but also in this world, in the misery, the cross, of human beings and their world.

Christians understand this entry of God into the world as a proof of God's unconditional love for human beings and as redemption, because through it the gulf between divine perfection and human imperfection, between life and death, has been overcome. And not just for the lifetime of Jesus of Nazareth: Christians believe that the God-man continues to be present and effective through the Spirit of God and that he continues to be a brotherly companion of men and women: to the power of the Father and the solidarity of the Son is added the abiding comfort of the Spirit.

Following the inner logic of this transformation of the image of God, for Christians God is 'threefold'. Here, too, apparent contradictions are held together, and as a result the sphere of Christian faith and thought comprises a very high degree of reality: a strict monotheism is combined with the threeness of 'Father', 'Son' and 'Spirit' in the one God.

Titles and dignities

'Jesus Christ' is used today as though it were a first name and a second name. In fact 'Jesus' is the given name for the man from Nazareth, while 'Christ' is a title through which the followers of Jesus express their recognition of him as the 'Messiah'.

'Christ' is the Greek translation of the Hebrew 'Messiah' and means 'anointed'. By this Jews understood and still understand the end-time king of the creation as consummated by God. In the New Testament this title is first used from the perspective after Jesus' death and resurrection.

The Old Testament book of Daniel (chapter 7) uses the title 'Son of Man' for the king who is the eternal ruler of the endtime, who comes on the clouds of heaven and is appointed to office by God himself. In the New Testament this title is used for Jesus only in the Gospels, where it is confined to the sayings of Jesus himself. Whether Jesus used it himself in this way is a controversial question.

'Servant of God' refers to texts in the Book of Isaiah (chapter 53) in which God's elect has to lead a life of shame and suffering. Christians very soon understood this passage in Isaiah as a prophecy of Jesus and attempted to explain the scandal of an executed Messiah by it.

'Son of God': in the Jewish tradition the king is sometimes

called Son of God (in the sense of an adopted son, see e.g. Psalm 2), but the pious are also called sons and daughters of God. If we reflect how consistently Jesus calls God his Father, we can also see this as a point of contact. In the writings of contemporary Hellenistic Jews, the world between God and human beings was populated by many kinds of intermediate beings without the strict monotheism of Judaism being jeopardized. The demigods of pagan myths might seem to be a help towards understanding what was meant by 'Son of God', but in fact they are misleading, since Christian theology, too (though not always popular belief), has constantly maintained a monotheistic posiiton. The title 'Son of God' became the most important title for later Christian theology.

The attempt to think of the divine and the human in Jesus together led to many models of thought, and in the course of history it provoked dispute, persecution and division among Christians. Nevertheless 'christology' is and remains the heart of any Christian reflection on God and the world.

4

Steps which Led to the Church

The preaching and life-style of Jesus had to be 'translated' for the use of the later church. From the beginning this gave rise to a potential for conflict which time and again has mobilized forces for renewal in church history, in endlessly repeated controversies. Explosives in the foundations – that was to become an unmistakable characteristic of Christianity.

With the conviction that Jesus was the expected Messiah (= Christ), a new religion had come into the world. In contrast to Moses and Buddha before him and Muhammad after him, Jesus became not only the starting point but even the object of a new faith. Certainly neither he nor his companions had any intention of founding a religion during their lifetimes, but the dynamic of their conviction about the incarnate God made its own way.

Three steps were necessary for the new religious conviction gradually to be moulded into a viable social form: from the itinerant disciples of Jesus to settled communities; from the Jewish sect to the mission to the Gentiles; and from the imminent expectation of the kingdom of God to the church in the course of history. The assertion which is often made that Paul founded the church is quite incorrect. He played a special part in the middle of the three steps, the mission to the Gentiles, but there were already communities before him, and only after him did people really become aware that the kingdom of God would not come so soon.

Itinerant or settled?

Take no gold, nor silver, nor copper in your belts, no bag for your journey, nor two tunics, nor sandals, nor a staff . . .

> Gospel according to Matthew, Chapter 10

If anyone comes to me and does not hate his own father and mother and wife and children and brothers and sisters, yes and even his own life, he cannot be my disciple.

> Gospel according to Luke, Chapter 14

Someone said, 'I will follow you, Lord, but let me first say farewell to those at my home.' Jesus said to him, 'No one who puts his hand to the plough and looks back is fit for the kingdom of God.'

> Gospel according to Luke, Chapter 9

Jesus and his companions travelled around with no fixed abode. Following his example, until well into the first decades of Christianity there were still vagabond preachers who lived by a kind of superior begging. For a little sustenance and now and then a roof over their heads they preached, healed the sick and blessed their benefactors. The success of their preaching could have two effects: some of their audience joined the itinerant preachers, and others became local sympathizers, who gave lodging to the itinerant preachers when they returned.

We must remember that such a life-style presupposed quite an extreme view of life and led to it. Itinerant preachers were by no means unusual; there were also itinerant philosophers (the Cynics) and they were all radical defenders of homelessness and renunciation of possessions, thinking nothing of family, wife and children.

Numerous passages in the Gospels reflect this view of life with sometimes brutal clarity.

But what were those who remained at home to make of rules of this kind, even if they sympathized with the itinerant preachers? For them such rules were impracticable. It is among the great achievements of the beginnings of Christianity that it succeeded in translating the ethic of itinerant Jesus groups into an ethic of settled Christian communities. That was the only way in which the new faith could survive. In the communities an attempt was made to create from a way of life which by its volatility was meant to bear witness to the imminence of the kingdom of God a sphere in which what was expected could to some degree be practised in anticipation: brotherly and sisterly love, mutual help, hospitality and sharing possessions, in order to balance out the difference between rich and poor.

There has always been a dispute over what was lost in this 'translation'. It was not just in the first century that the two forms of Christianity lived side by side, especially as they were dependent on each other. Later, too, renewal movements constantly came into being which were opposed to an all-too-sedentary church and called for discipleship in the form in which Jesus himself had lived it: without possessions and without a home. Usually such reform movements then went through the same process: the founders were radical, but in order to keep the movement alive their successors had to sketch out rules and build houses, until they themselves in turn were confronted with new radical beginnings.

The story of an alienation

Jesus was a Jew and confessed Judaism without any qualifications. All those who went around the country with him were Jews as he was. And the Gospels do not conceal the fact that Jesus was aware of having been sent expressly to the Jewish people.

So when after Jesus' death the enthusiasm of belief in him also extended to non-Jews, a difficult problem arose: did Gentiles have first to become Jews in order to become Christians? At any rate this course was implicit in the logic of the development: earliest Christianity in fact understood itself as a Jewish group, indeed as the true Israel, for which the promises of the Bible had already been fulfilled. At first the conservative earliest community in Jerusalem did not diverge from this line: only those who were Jews or who were prepared to lead their lives in accordance with the rule of the Jewish tradition could become Christians. However, Paul, who was meanwhile already travelling in Asia Minor, was meeting more Gentiles than Jews, and they adhered to the new faith. Paul refused to compel these Gentiles to observe the Jewish laws of purity and circumcision. In particular it was his conversion experience that the precepts of the Jewish law, the Torah, which he himself had observed in a radical way, did not give him more freedom and did not bring him closer to God, but had only made him aware of the lack of freedom in human beings and of how remote they are from God. Whenever in the later history of Christianity rules and regulations again came to set the tone, there were similarly dramatic conversions (e.g. in the case of Luther); this fundamental departure from the traditional law also gave Christianity the opportunity of inculturation – it did not have to tie itself to its origins. But the question remained: how much of Judaism might be given up?

When in 48/49 (according to other reckonings perhaps as

early as 43/44) Paul was again in Jerusalem, there was conflict over communal meals. After much toing and froing – the controversy was later given the splendid name 'Apostolic Council' – agreement was reached on a two-tiered observance of the Torah, so as not to put excessive difficulties in the way of Gentiles who had found their way to belief in Christ. This set the seal first on a parallel co-existence of Jewish Christians and Gentile Christians and then on a rift between them, leading to a great landmark: a subsequent split between Jews and Christians. Now that Gentiles were mixing with Christians and in many places formed the overwhelming majority, they posed an insoluble problem to the Jewish Christians, who still saw themselves as Jews. How were they were to keep fellowship if they could not even sit at the same table because of the food laws?

The rift was only patched up at the so-called Apostolic Council. The destruction of Jerusalem in 70 drove both Jews and Jewish Christians from the city. Three decades later (at the Synod of Jabneh, 100) the Jews excluded all 'false believers', including the Jewish Christians, from the synagogue. There are said to have been Jewish–Christian communities in Arabia until the sixth century, and some historians conjecture that Muhammad came to know Christianity through them.

As a result of its resolute mission to the Gentiles, Christianity took the way towards becoming a universal world religion. From then on the decisive factor for this religion was no longer membership of this or that people, but solely a shared faith. Like the frontiers between peoples, so too the frontiers of class and gender fell – at least this was the claim; the degree to which universalism often remained vague theory is a dark chapter in church history. At any rate we can read in an old baptismal formula in Paul: 'There is neither Jew nor Greek, there is neither slave nor free, there is neither male nor female . . .' (Gal.3.28).

From the Declaration of the Second Vatican Council on the Relation of the Church to Non-Christian Religions (1965)

'Remembering her common heritage with the Jews and moved not by any political consideration, but solely by the religious motivation of Christian charity, the church deplores all hatreds, persecutions, displays of antisemitism levelled at any time and from any source against the Jews.'

Nostra aetate, 4

But this achievement had a dark side. The drifting apart of Jewish Christians and Gentile Christians turned the opposition between Christians and Jews into a factor which caused bitterness among Christians about an origin which they liked less and less. The history of this alienation was still vivid to the authors of the New Testament as a conflict which they had just experienced. Paul struggles with the question how salvation can have passed over from the Jews, i.e. his own people, to the Gentiles. Dispute and mutual repudiation then become manifest in the Gospels in a harsh vocabulary which often amounts to propaganda.

Distinctions vanish, the Pharisees are portrayed simply as opponents of Jesus, and the last Gospel, that of John, speaks only of 'the Jews' who reject the message of Jesus. Hence the anti-Jewish passages in the New Testament which were misused by later generations to legitimate all kinds of attacks on Jews.

Enmity against the Jews is an early and momentous lapse within Christianity. It is only in our century, after the Holocaust, that a new understanding of the way in which Christian faith originated in Jewish faith has developed.

The return postponed

'*There are some standing here who will not taste death before they see the kingdom of God come with power.*'

Gospel according to Mark, Chapter 9

The expectation that the end-time kingdom of God was imminent, indeed the conviction that it had already come, was the heart of the message with which Jesus went through Palestine. It was the understanding that Jesus himself was the first new man in this kingdom of God that allowed the Jesus movement to survive after the death of its master. However, as a result the expectation that there would not be long to wait before the end of this world and the beginning of a new one had by no means been quenched. Jesus had inculcated this expectation into his followers all too often. The many announcements of the end time made in the New Testament reflect this side of Jesus' teaching and at the same time say something about the expectations of the Christian communities at the time when the New Testament texts were composed. The later the texts, the greater the problem: how much longer was there to wait? When would the Risen Christ come again and reshape the whole world?

Paul (I Thess.4.13–17; I Cor.15.51) believes that the return of Jesus is still to be expected during his lifetime, and defends this hope against the doubters in communities which are witnessing the death of many Christians before they experience the great event. The later writings no longer reckon with an end to the world in the foreseeable future; this brings to the fore the question of the attitude that needs to be taken to the world, now and in the future.

Here a further step was necessary: the historical approach of the Jewish Bible (the 'Old Testament'), which was directed towards an end time of salvation, at first seemed to be fulfilled in Jesus, even if his death – as a painful interruption – was for a short time holding up the headlong course of the world towards its end. But then, when the short time became a long one and seemed never ending, this interruption led to a new dialectical concept of history: the time of salvation has already begun, but it is not yet completed. Eschatology, the doctrine of the last things, split into two halves, a present and a futuristic eschatology. In essence everything has already happened now; death and injustice, suffering and finitude, have already been overcome (by the death and resurrection of Jesus), but the new world is not yet definitively visible. Therefore it is necessary to wait for a second, future end of time, the date of which the New Testament does not indicate in any way.

In his First Letter to the Corinthians (Chapter 7), Paul develops an ethic for the intermediate period before the return of Christ:

'Brethren, the appointed time has grown very short; from now on, let those who have wives live as though they had none, and those who mourn as though they were not mourning, and those who rejoice as though they were not rejoicing, and those who buy as though they had no goods, and those who deal with the world as though they had no dealing with it. For the form of this world is passing away.'

With this second expectation Christians thought and think just like Jews; both religions live in the 'not yet'. But Christians find the first conviction, that the time of salvation has already begun, very difficult to defend in arguments. 'What has changed in the world after almost 2000 years?', they are asked by Jews and other non-Christians. In what does the 'already now' of the end time which has already dawned consist? Down to the present this question has become a further topic of theological and philosophical reflection which will not be silenced, and provides material for every conceivable model of religious criticism and anticlericalism.

At the end of the first century the most important attempt to cope with the problem of the postponement of the end time and the return of Christ was also made in literary form, in the Apocalypse, or Revelation of John. Since then this last book of the New Testament has prompted numerous speculations; it has become the favourite readings of cabals and sects and even now disseminates a terror which was later illustrated by Hieronymus Bosch. However, for Bosch the comparative restraint of the Johannine apocalypse was not enough. and what he depicted was the bloodier notions of apocryphal texts (texts outside the Bible). In reality things are quite simple.

Apocalyptic notions, with gruesome imagery depicting the final struggle between the powers of good and the powers of evil, had been widespread since the time of the Maccabees, and were applied to any natural catastrophe, any social and political revolution, any persecution; in particular, the destruction of Jerusalem and the temple nurtured the certainty that things could not go on as they were much longer. Many Christians had the same conviction, above all when the first massive Roman persecutions of Christians began. The question was: how was one now to come to terms with a world which was already in its death throes?

The Revelation of John gives the following answer to this. First of all, the Christian communities must be concerned with the present and lead a respectable life here and now. Very much to the incomprehension of all who engage in speculation, Revelation in fact begins with three chapters of firm admonitions to seven Christian churches in Asia Minor. Secondly, any imminent expectation, i.e. the hope of a speedy return of the Messiah Jesus, must be abandoned; but the consciousness of living in an intermediate period must not be lost, even if this intermediate period lasts for millennia.

Three steps were the necessary presupposition for the gradual development of the new religious conviction into a church:

The radical ethic of the itinerant disciples of Jesus had to be translated for the use of settled communities;

The small Jewish sect had to leave its origins behind and disseminate its conviction as a universal doctrine of salvation;

The imminent expectation of the kingdom of God had to be abandoned in favour of a more 'divided' notion of the end time: the beginning of the end is Jesus as Christ, but the end is still to come.

5

Persecution and Expansion

Christianity has to be understood in the light of the tensions which shaped it in the first three centuries. Two thousand years of the history of this religion have developed as a series of constantly repeated variations on some basic themes which were struck up at the beginning.

Exercises in assimilation

The first communities certainly did not have what was later to be called 'church order', and while Paul organized them and assigned tasks here and there, he showed a remarkable lack of interest in any kind of hierarchical structure, even where he speaks of ministries: no statutes were needed for a brief transitional period. On the one hand the authority of the apostles, who had known Jesus, was still undisputed, and on the other a quasi-democratic order followed from the fact that initially all those who joined this new religion did so out of conviction.

This changed in the next generation. Already at that time not only individuals who had converted were baptized, but also whole 'houses': families with children and domestic servants. Once the hope of a speedy end to the world had vanished, people looked on the world with different eyes. Christians still had no hesitation in propagating an executed Messiah – 'a stumbling block to Jews and folly to Gentiles', as Paul writes (I Cor.1.23) – but they began to seek recognition in respectable society. Talk had gone the rounds about the craziness of Christian worship, which had been inflated to make it notorious: there were ecstatic outbursts, stammering prophets, and even women speaking in public! That was all right for a sect living in the last days, but for a church on its way through history all at once something quite different became important: a good image.

In the late letters of the New Testament, which certainly were not written by Paul himself, though they are in his name (I Timothy, II Timothy, Titus), prayer is already being called for 'for rulers and all who are in high positions, that we may lead a quiet and peaceable life' (I Tim.2.2). What a difference from the radical view of life among the itinerant preachers! Now assimilation was the order of the day; now no offence was to be caused to society; now the Christians had to be seen to be respectable citizens. This also included a new, assimilated role for women. In the Jesus movement and in the first decades of earliest Christianity women had been accredited ambassadors of the new faith: they held office, preached and went on missionary journeys. Fifty years later we can read in the First Letter to Timothy: 'Let a woman learn in silence with all submissiveness. I permit no woman to teach . . .' (I Tim.2.11f.).

The persecutions, which intensified and kept recurring, were an ever more urgent reason for attempting not to attract attention. They already began with the emperor Nero (54–68), to whose childish cruelty presumably Peter and Paul also fell victim. Three further great persecutions of Christians under the emperors Septimus Severus (193–211), Decius (249–51) and Diocletian (284–305) were only the climaxes of a varied history of suffering which gave early Christianity countless martyrs. At the same time there was no stopping the new religion. At the end of the second century there was a distinguished catechetical school in Alexandria and there were 100 bishops throughout Egypt. A Roman synod around 250 brought together 60 bishops from Italy, and when Cyprian of Carthage summoned an assembly of the North African churches in 256, 87 bishops were his guests. At this time one could already point to numerous Christian communities in Spain and Gaul, in Arabia and India.

The fight against Gnosticism

A strange movement occupied early Christianity for almost five centuries; scholars are still not agreed on its origins. This was Gnosticism, a fellowship of the 'enlightened' which branched out in all directions. This shimmering 'wave of esotericism' with its many forms already began in the New Testament period: a mixture of Christian, Jewish and pagan elements became the secret religion of people who felt that they had been chosen, and for whom current religious notions were too ordinary.

Gnostics were not easy to identify: they seemed to fit in wherever they appeared because in any case they felt that they were above existing doctrines and the primitive practice of established rites. Nevertheless, they were not simply superior individualists, but had a particular attitude in common.

Only a few decades ago it was difficult to grasp what Gnosticism was all about, because almost everything to do with it had to be reconstructed from the attacks on the Gnostics in Christian writings. However, in 1945 a farmer in Upper Egypt discovered clay jars at Nag Hammadi in which 13 volumes containing 51 works in Coptic amounting to 1130 pages had been concealed. These were Gnostic texts, and they allow us some insight into the thought system of this movement.

For the Gnostics, a particular myth explained the disastrous state of the world: all human beings have the divine spark in their souls, but not everyone is aware of it. The 'portion of God' in human beings pines in the prison of the body. Sophia, the heavenly wisdom, is to blame for this: in an attack of lasciviousness she gave birth to the demiurge, a monster for whom there was no place in heaven. Consequently the demiurge created his own abode: the world as it is now, a world of uncertainty and violence, of foolishness and desire. Human beings have to bear the consequences of the heavenly dispute, and only those who know all about it and moreover remain childless, i.e. give the demiurge no new 'prisons for the sparks', have an opportunity of getting where they belong, to the divine world.

For some contemporaries in the first centuries Gnosticism fitted the spirit of the age better than Christianity. In turbulent times it is difficult to believe in the good creator; the sense of being the elite in a secret group seemed to be an intellectual gain, and the creative mixture of themes from different religions gave rise to a 'new-age feeling' of free choice and better perception.

In the battle against Gnosticism, Christianity lost the mood of its earliest days – this too is one of the elements which shaped the early history of this religion and led to a deep-seated anxiety about ideological infiltration. Now the desire was for 'sound teaching', and in the face of the Gnostics and their hostility to children this meant that 'woman will be saved by bearing children' (I Tim.2.15). In the eyes of educated pagans an early Puritanism, coupled with a popular anti-intellectualism, gave Christianity the appearance of being moralistic and antiquated. On the other hand, at that time, in a remarkable intellectual achievement, Christianity assimilated ancient Greek and contemporary philosophy through its learned representatives (the 'church fathers'). This very move, combined with its high moral standards, was to predestine the religion of the crucified redeemer, after many persecutions, for a role as a new spiritual power which would support the state.

The shift under Constantine

When the emperor Constantine came to power and in 313, in the Edict of Milan, decided to give Christians freedom, his motives were not just tolerance and philanthropy. The Roman state ideology had undergone many changes. After the polytheism of the Republic and a fluctuation between syncretistic tolerance and compulsory observance of the central cult of Jupiter, finally the emperor himself had become the divine symbol which held the empire together. The fact that the Christians did not take part in the emperor cult had been a constant occasion for their persecution. But the deepest concern was to find one idea of the state in the one empire, to achieve consensus in basic ethical and religious values as the precondition for the viability of the enormous multinational and multicultural structure which the Roman empire now represented. Constantine realized that only a radical change to the previous policy could restore the cohesion which had become so fragile: Christianity, which hitherto had constantly been regarded as a danger to the state, was itself gradually to be made its ideological foundation. That not only helped the Roman state but neutralized Christianity, because it shared the responsibility.

Constantine's insight here was his great political achievement. Sixty years later, in 380, once Christianity had been tolerated and given an equal status, the emperor Theodosius went one step further and finally made it the state religion. Now it was the pagans who were persecuted. Thus there began an era, full of conflict, in which church and state were associated; it was to shape the face of Christianity for 1500 years to come.

The dynamic of the development of Christianity is powered by an alternating emphasis on opposing tendencies:

a settled middle-class existence –
renunciation of home, possessions and family;

links back to tiny Jewish Palestine –
a claim to world-wide validity;

an imminent expectation of the end of the world –
the formation of institutions and traditions;

assimilation to society –
resistance as an alternative society;

Political subversiveness –
legitimation of power.

Thus very different trends could develop within Christianity, all of which appeal to the New Testament and the tradition of the first period; that is why in this religion the dispute over authorities and institutions which determine what is right has so great a significance.

6

Under the Pantocrator

The lordly Christ, depicted larger than life in the apses of the churches of late antiquity as Pantocrator (ruler of all), is not just of interest for the history of art. In this type of image, which replaced the representations of the Good Shepherd, we can see a changed relationship between Christianity and political power.

The new freedom for Christians changed not only the political landscape but also Christians' view of their own religion. The place of the emperor worshipped in the pagan period as divine was taken by the God-man, but in an imperious pose, and the real emperor understood himself as Christ's earthly representative. Thus Christian criticism of a divinization of the emperor turned into the divine legitimation of imperial power. From then on, emperors and kings 'by the grace of God' ruled in Europe.

A religion becomes political

The development of Christianity from permitted religion to compulsory religion was interrupted only briefly, in the reign of the emperor Julian (361–363). He wanted to inaugurate a renaissance of the Roman tradition and encouraged pagan cults.

As a result, Christian historians called him 'the apostate'. Theodosius the Great (379–395) put an end to such attempts by making Christianity the state religion – a logical step, since the new religion was to serve to legitimate the imperial power, and therefore the rivalry of other religions had inevitably to be regarded as a cause of political uncertainty.

When Theodosius died in 395, the progressive disintegration of the Roman empire was marked politically, and the empire was divided into a western half (with Rome as its capital) and an eastern half (the capital of which was Constantinople/Byzantium, present-day Istanbul). From the fifth to the seventh centuries the East played the pioneer role. All the councils of the early church took place on eastern territory, and here the dominant position of the emperor over the church which had begun with Constantine was established. The model of 'Caesaropapism' accorded the emperor a role in church government, because – as a development of the pagan imperial cult – he was regarded as God's image and co-regent even during his lifetime. As a result, state laws could also be given religious sanction. The Byzantine treasury was called 'the most holy fiscus', and withholding of tax could be punished as a religious offence. In succession to the East Roman/Byzantine emperors (after the capture of Constantinople by the Ottomans in 1453), the Russian Czar took over not only the title of emperor but also the role of supreme head of the Orthodox church, and the role of Russian Orthodoxy within the state even after the October Revolution of 1917 can be explained not least from the almost unbroken tradition of this model of the state church.

The papacy as a power factor

The development in the Western Roman church followed quite a different course. A few decades after the division of the empire, the power of the emperor had declined to such an extent that the pope in Rome became the last real political figure in Italy. Pope Leo the Great (440–461) was the one who convinced Attila king of the Huns to withdraw in 452, and he was at least able to persuade Geiserich, king of the Goths, not to burn down Rome, even if he did plunder it. In 476 the last West Roman emperor, Romulus Augustulus, was finally expelled by the Germanic mercenary leader Odovaker; by then the other provinces of the West Roman empire, Britain, Gaul, Spain, North Africa, etc., had long been over-run by the migrations of the Goths and Huns, the Vandals, Franks and Langobards.

In these circumstances, caesaropapism could not develop in Rome. On the contrary, the political power which had fallen to the popes as the only guarantors of legitimacy and tradition became the foundation of a claim to political power that saw itself always as at least an equivalent counterpart to the 'secular' power of the European emperors and kings, and very often also as a superior authority.

Thus the political weakness in the fifth century gave rise to a politically powerful papacy, and as a result to a dual model of the 'spiritual' and the 'secular', of 'two kingdoms' (Augustine, died 430) or 'two powers' (Pope Gelasius I, 492–496). The whole development of Western history is stamped by this antagonism between church and state; that is also the only explanation for the rise of a church state, which in the form of the Roman Vatican state is still even now an entity in international law.

The sovereign political self-understanding of the Roman Catholic church, the way in which it swings between political coalitions and political resistance, which even now is a factor in current disputes within the church, has its roots here.

Initially, the papacy as a power factor was welcome to the inhabitants of Italy, because in times of complete collapse in Europe it could at least guarantee a minimum of political stability. And subsequently, the new European peoples also benefited from this development. This was not only because they increasingly became Christian. As the new authorities, they were based on the territory of the Roman empire, and though this no longer existed, only the Roman pope could legitimize their power, where this was felt important, in succession to the former Roman emperor. The empire had indeed served its purpose, but it was, and for centuries continued to be, useful to be able to show that one was one of its heirs.

Charlemagne in Rome: the Middle Ages

Historians make the Christian Middle Ages begin at different dates, but at the latest with the year 800. Why?

Charles, king of the Franks, short in stature and later nicknamed 'the Great', Charlemagne, had a sense of history and round dates. In the forty-six years of his rule the kingdom of the Franks became the new Western great power and comprised all the Germanic tribes.

After five hundred years of migration, the tribes which had entered the Mediterranean area from the north and the east had by and large reached their final abodes. They generally adopted Christianity along with the Hellenistic life-style of late antiquity. In the east, Islam had arisen as a new religion (the Islamic reckoning of time begins with the emigration of the prophet Muhammad from Mecca in 622); in an unprecedented series of victories, within the space of a century it had conquered Arabia and Persia, North African and Spain. East Roman Byzantium, already damaged by the migrations, was now further reduced by the Muslim Arabs and only held the Balkan peninsula and Asia Minor.

In this situation the new order in Europe lacked only symbolic legitimation through history. Charles was aware of this and acted. On Christmas Day 800 he was in Rome and had himself crowned emperor by Pope Leo III. There had been no West Roman emperor for more than 300 years, and the return of this title enabled the king of the Franks to claim to be king of the kings of Europe and to be restoring the old unity of the empire in the West.

Byzantium protested, but fell into line twelve years later, and recognized the new Western emperor. At the same time the political recognition of the pope was connected with this; as a result he was put in the position of making European politics for a full millennium as the broker of imperial power.

Against this background the mediaeval Christianity of the West developed on two levels: church politics, caught in the tug-of-war between emperor and pope, was a factor in conflicts right down to those between bishops and local rulers, clergy and landowners.

Religious movements very often ran across the lines of church politics, attacking a politicized church; they were fought against as heresy or integrated as impulses towards reform. The frame of reference and the criterion for the controversies is the notion of a universal order in which the idea of the ancient Roman empire is promoted to become an element in Christian salvation history. But it was above all the interests and claims of the universal powers (emperor and pope) that could be fitted into this idealistic superstructure, and not so much the efforts of peripheral areas and regions towards autonomy. Political and religious centralism competed with each other, formed the motive power of European history, and at the same time reduced it to ever smaller units as a result of an endless chain of bloody conflicts. That Christianity did not completely lose its credibility as a result of its political ambitions and collapse is something that it owes to its heretics and saints, who persistently restored the links to the time of the beginnings, before Constantine.

After the recognition of Christianity, the new state religion could no longer dissociate itself from political developments. In Byzantium the emperor directed church policy; the fact that in the West the pope had political responsibility for centuries made Roman Christianity more political than its origins warranted.

7

Politics and Theological Disputes

The close links between the church and politics, once Christianity had become the imperial religion of the Roman empire, led to political interests being transferred to every theological dispute and becoming a factor. The very first council of the early church also provided the first example of this.

The councils

It was neither the Roman pope nor one of the Eastern patriarchs ('archbishop' over several dioceses) who summoned the first council in church history. Rather, the emperor Constantine, now that he had designated Christianity the religion of the empire, felt compelled to intervene in the theological disputes and introduce some order.

He commanded the bishops of the whole empire to appear in Nicaea (in Asia Minor, on the coast of the Sea of Marmara) in May 325, treated them like imperial officials, allowed them to travel by the imperial post and saw to it that they spent two months in discussion there. He himself gave the opening speech, declared the council resolutions to be imperial laws, and combined the conclusion of the council in July with a splendid banquet to mark the twentieth anniversary of his reign.

All the ancient councils followed this model. The emperors always took the initiative, and even Charlemagne still summoned councils. The question how far the church could make 'free' decisions here is an anachronistic one,

List of councils

Number	Year	Place

The seven ecumenical councils of antiquity

1	325	Nicaea (1)
2	381	Constantinople (1)
3	431	Ephesus
4	451	Chalcedon
5	553	Constantinople (2)
6	680/1	Constantinople (3)
7	787	Nicaea (2)

The disputed eighth council

8	869/70	Constantinople (4)
	879/80	Rival council of the Eastern church

The seven papal councils of the Western church in the high Middle Ages

9	1123	Rome/Lateran (1)
10	1139	Rome/Lateran (2)
11	1179	Rome/Lateran (3)
12	1215	Rome/Lateran (4)
13	1245	Lyons (1)
14	1274	Lyons (2)
15	1311/12	Vienne

The three councils which attempted church reform in the West

16	1414/18	Constance
17	1438/45	Basel/Ferrara/Florence
18	1512/17	Rome/Lateran (5)

The three councils of the Roman Catholic church after the Reformation

19	1545/63	Trent
20	1869/70	Rome/Vatican (1)
21	1962/65	Rome/Vatican (2)

from a time when the mediaeval popes were very much on
the defensive against imperial church politics. The collaboration of laity, in this case the emperor and also the empress
and their officials, in church decisions was general, and it
was only in the nineteenth and twentieth centuries that the
Roman Catholic church gave this up in favour of complete
clericalization.

That did not prevent the councils from setting the
direction for a new and more precise version of Christian
faith. Above all the first four councils in the period of
roughly 150 years after Constantine's edict of tolerance
were decisive here. The occasion was always what theologians call 'christology'. In its new, recognized position
Christianity was very much in need of explanation, above
all in connection with two questions.

- Had not Christianity diverged from strict biblical
  monotheism in believing not only in a Father God but
  also in a Son God and a divine Spirit? The notion of a
  threefold God (Trinity) was not only a problem for Jews
  (and later Muslims); it was also difficult to translate into
  the categories of contemporary philosophical thought.

- How could a human being, Jesus, be said at the same time
  to be God, without either deifying a human being or
  reducing God to the human level, as a result of which by
  definition he would cease to be God?

The Alexandrian monk and priest Arius (died 336) put
forward the view that only one, namely the Father, could be
God; the Son was a creature of the Father, and the Spirit a
creature of the Son. The Council of Nicaea (325) rejected
this model and declared that Father and Son were 'of the
same substance' (the terms 'of the same substance' and 'of
similar substance' differ by only one letter in Greek). The
subsequent Council of Constantinople (381) also rejected

all compromises on this question. The creed of Nicaea in the version approved by the First Council of Constantinople is still common to Orthodox, Catholic and Protestant churches. However, at that time these decisions did not prevent the emperor Constantine and his successor from continuing to support the Arian side; Arianism gained ground among both Goths and Germans and for some centuries was the most widespread species of Christianity.

A century after Nicaea another version of the question stood at the centre. In the view of a certain Nestorius (he died in 451), who came from Antioch and became patriarch of Constantinople, one could not call Mary mother of God (Greek *theotokos*) because she had brought only the human being Jesus into the world. Cyril (died 444), patriarch of Alexandria, opposed this because it would mean that Jesus had not been God right from the beginning. The dispute was carried on by every possible means and was not least also a dispute about the political pre-eminence of the two patriarchs. Finally the emperor Theodosius II summoned a council at Ephesus in 431. The piquancy of this lay in the fact that not only could Ephesus (on the Aegean coast of Asia Minor) offer a great church dedicated to Mary as a meeting place (a legend relates that Mary died in Ephesus), but previously it had been the city of the great mother goddess Artemis and, just as it had previously lived on pilgrimage to her, now lived on the increasing veneration of Mary.

The council decided against Nestorius: he was deposed and exiled. That was consistent theologically, and although the issue was how it was possible to think about the God-man Jesus Christ, what proved almost more decisive for the history of Christian piety was that now Mary could in fact be called 'mother of God'. From then on, those who venerated Mary, from the Middle Ages to the present day, could depict the mother of Jesus in such a way that sometimes – certainly not according to church teaching, but *de facto* – she became a fourth divine person over and above the Trinity.

One result of the council was a further permanent split in the church. However, the Council of Ephesus by no means resolved the question how God and man could be thought of together in Jesus Christ. In combating the teaching of Nestorius his opponents overshot the mark by now thinking of the divine and human natures as combined in such a way that only one was left: the divine nature. Accordingly, those who held this view were called 'Monophysites'. The emperor Marcian, or more precisely his powerful wife Pulcheria, summoned a council for 451 in Chalcedon (on the Bosphorus, opposite Constantinople). It became the greatest council before Vatican I in 1870 and condemned Monophysitism.

The consequence was the third great split in the church. Five 'ancient Eastern' churches round the eastern Mediterranean from Egypt to Armenia did not recognize the decisions of the council. The deeper reason for their rejection of them lay in political and cultural developments whch had already gradually shattered the fragile unity of the Mediterranean area in the fifth century.

The formula by which christology was given its classic and definitive intellectual expression at Chalcedon is of far-reaching significance in two respects. It speaks of the full divinity and the full humanity in Jesus Christ, i.e. of two natures which are 'unconfused and unchangeable, indivisible and inseparable'. Here was the establishment of on the one hand a dialectical way of thinking, i.e. a way of thinking orientated on the combination of two permanent opposites, and on the other hand of the use of negative terms. Both these were the foundation for a high standard of thinking in Christian theology and a respect for its own limits – characteristics which were to go on to govern the European intellectual tradition. Other questions, too, were solved along the lines of this model – for example the dilemma of freedom and predestination which preoccupied the greatest theologian of antiquity, Augustine (died 430); so the church-political antagonism of the West had a rational instrument at its disposal which it took up time and again.

The great schism

Nestorians and Monophysites had already turned their back on church unity. And by the end of the first millennium the Western and Eastern churches had come to live so far apart that a trivial occasion was enough to introduce the break. Political differences contributed another factor: Byzantium still held territories in the south of the Italian peninsula, and this ran counter to the growing political claims of the popes. But the real reason for the break was the dispute over the primacy of the pope.

Two centuries after Charlemagne, the pendulum swing between the pre-eminence of the popes and that of the emperors, so typical of the West, had moved to the imperial side. The emperors after Otto I (936–973) surrounded themselves with increasing sacral splendour, and Otto III (983–1002) sought to re-establish the Roman empire based on Rome. By contrast the papacy had been weakened and was disputed.

In 1046, at the Synod of Sutri, Henry III had to depose three popes who had been elected by different parties and appoint a fourth. This nadir was a turning point; the reform movement in the church, directed against misuse of office and priestly marriages, which had emanated from the monastery of Cluny in Burgundy, was promoted by subsequent popes. The self-assurance of the popes grew again.

A climax in the ideological controversy was the *Dictatus papae* of 1075, a document which laid claim to the unlimited supreme rule and jurisdiction of the pope over the whole church, and further the inerrancy of the pope in spiritual questions and his authority to depose emperors. This set out a programme for church politics which, while it removed many actual abuses, was also a programme for new conflicts.

One of the most ardent advocates of church reform was Humbert, a monk in Lothringia and later cardinal bishop. In documents and speeches he stormed against laity who bestowed spiritual offices, against clergy who bought such offices, in short against anything which could be interpreted as intervention in the unlimited rights of the papacy.

The most resolute opponents of the papal claim to supremacy over all the church were of course to be found in Constantinople/Byzantium. In the summer of 1054 a delegation travelled East for negotiations; Humbert was its leader. In Byzantium he met the patriarch Michael Cerularius, who was not prepared to bow to any wishes from Rome; Humbert for his part had no intention of returning home without having settled things.

That sealed the break: on 16 July, Humbert set down the bull of excommunication in Hagia Sophia, the church of the patriarchate of Byzantium; five days later the patriarch excluded from the church all Romans who had excluded him. Each side attributed every conceivable heresy to the other. The great schism between the Eastern church (which calls itself the right believing = Orthodox church) and the Western church (which calls it the Catholic = universal church) still exists.

'Division of labour' in a monopolistic religion

In its first millennium, what was formerly a new religion had moved a long way from its beginnings. At the price of a close link with the state and politics it had become the monopoly religion of all Europe. No one could not belong to it; only Jews had an endangered exceptional position, and they were tolerated, restricted, persecuted, expelled, and tolerated again, depending on the political opportunity. Everything that ran counter to the postulate of the Christian unity of the continent, indeed of the whole Mediterranean area, was experienced as a severe identity crisis and combated with increasingly harsh means.

The ongoing political theme of emperor and pope put those not directly involved in it in the shade. Regional interests gradually began to assert themselves in France and England, in northern and eastern Europe, and it was rarely possible to separate the religious from the political points of reference. What from a political perspective was regionalism was in religious terms a multiplicity of languages, mentalities and forms of life seeking to find expression. In addition, reference was constantly made to the beginnings, because it was all too evident that a pope residing in pomp in Rome, a maker of international policies, could hardly be understood as the representative of that Jesus of Nazareth who had lived without means and had become a victim of politics. A monopoly religion is always at the mercy of such contradictions; only a far-reaching 'division of labour' seems to make it possible to live with it.

The first 'division of labour' was the formation of different states in the church: clergy and laity. There was already a contrast in the New Testament period between Christians who held office and those who did not, but it was the adaptation of this to a society organized through and through in states and the elevation of clergy to the rank of imperial officials that first made this contrast a two-class society, even if the inner frontier within it was much easier to cross than other barriers of class. One reason for this was the obligation to celibacy, which had been constantly inculcated in priests since the fourth century and which despite all opposition gradually came to be established after the Cluny reform. Thus no hereditary dynasties of priests could develop, for every new priest came from the lay state. Because for a long time not all Christians had been living, or could live, by the standards of the gospel, the division between clergy and laity resulted in a kind of reciprocal representation: the former were responsible for prayer and worship, the latter for business, war and procreation.

A 'division of labour' among the clergy which has continued to the present day involves the relationship between the teaching office, the magisterium, and theology, above all in the Roman Catholic church. Already at the councils of the ancient church the bishops claimed the right to make decisions in questions of doctrine, and in order to do that they needed, as they still do today, the professional competence of theologians. The centralization of even doctrinal decisions in the Western church by the pope very often made this 'division of labour' a battleground. The problem that proved almost unsurmountable was and is that a scriptural religion which is two thousand years old has accumulated an enormous mass of tradition that only specialists can work on; on the other hand the faith of Christians is a question of conviction, as at the beginning, and not of theological study. The inevitable conflict between knowledge and faith still makes headlines today.

A third 'division of labour' in the sphere of a monopolistic religion is still the contrast between normal (parish) communities, in which the majority of Christians live, and the communities of monks and nuns in monasteries and convents. For centuries, committed Christians had the serious alternative of living in the world or in the cloister. The first Christian communities had attempted to shape an alternative model to society; in the sphere of their common life peace, love and the sharing of possessions were to be the rule. A monopolistic religion to which everyone belongs is not in a position to live out its own alternative model. So representative monastic orders took over this task and thus salvaged some of the claims from the early period for the mainstream church.

Monks and nuns

Christian monasticism originated in Egypt. Individual enthusiasts withdrew as anchorites (solitaries) or hermits (dwellers in the wilderness) to a life of strict asceticism and uncompromising flight from the world. Antony (died 356) is regarded as one of their founders. Struck by the story of the rich young man (who was unwilling to give up his possessions to follow Jesus, Matt.19.16–26), he is said to have resolved on a solitary monastic life. Even during his lifetime, Antony, the desert father, was the goal of pilgrimage by people seeking his advice. At around the same time the monastic father Pachomius (292–346) established another model of monastic life: the cenobites (= those living in community) advocated a monastic life with strict rules instead of solitude. Pachomius, who before his conversion was a pagan soldier, required his monks to observe lifelong celibacy, to give up all private possessions, and to show strict obedience – military virtues which brought him success. In the end he was administering eleven monasteries in the great Nile delta which exported their craftsmanship and agricultural products downstream to Alexandria with their own fleet on the Nile.

Communal life in the monastery became established as the model of a Christian society in the Eastern and Western churches. Very soon 'virgins and widows', who had been regarded as a separate state in the early church, came together to share a monastic life. Women's orders were often at the same time a refuge and a place of retirement for unmarried female relations; however, they also offered women the freedom to develop and to engage in cultural, academic and charitable work extending far beyond the possibilities of those who had to live under the tutelage of father or husband.

The West, more sober and less radically ascetic, took two centuries longer to produce the first great founder of a religious order, Benedict of Nursia (in Perugia, 480–547). Benedict studied in Rome, had enough of big city life, spent three years as hermit in a cave near Subiaco, finally gathered a hermit community about himself, and settled with them around 529 on Monte Cassino, where he wrote the rule of his order. Monte Cassino is still – after much destruction, from the Langobards to the Second World War – the oldest Western monastery.

For long stretches of Christian history men's and women's orders were spiritual centres and vehicles of culture, but they also often lost their function and died out. The Reformation opposed them on the grounds that men and women cannot justify themselves in their own strength before God, even with self-imposed asceticism. The Enlightenment attacked monasteries on the grounds that society has no use for the prayer and fasting of such outsiders.

The number of Western religious communities up to the present day (including those which have died out and been dissolved) is estimated at around 4000. Through the variety of their rules, their ways of life and their tasks, they also met something of the need for pluralism in the framework of the one monopoly religion. The representative function of the monastery becomes clear from the fact that above all those Christians who did not live in a monastery, whether clergy or laity, regarded it as an act particularly well pleasing to God to found and endow a monastery. The radical features of the demands made by the gospel, which could not be denied even in a monopolistic religion, were transferred to monks and nuns in order to relieve 'ordinary Christians' in their average parish communities of the need to meet them. Along the same lines, the saints are not only models for believers to imitate but are also often felt to be so above them that their veneration also serves to secure those religious 'merits' which ordinary Christians cannot obtain for themselves.

Heretics and saints

The spiritual movements which arose in the five hundred years between the two great schisms – from 1054 to Luther's Reformation in 1517 – can all be said to follow the same pattern. First comes opposition to the form of Christianity as it is lived in a particular present; a return to the beginnings is called for and practised; the clerical church reacts defensively; in a usually tedious controversy the new movement is either accused of heresy and persecuted, or accepted as a reform movement and integrated into the church as a 'division of labour'. Which alternative is followed depends on the view of church leaders as to how far the new movement endangers the theological or organizational foundations of the monopolistic mainstream church.

Here, by way of examples of this problem in the Western church, are two cases from the history of the high Middle Ages:

• In the 1170s, the rich merchant Peter Waldo (died 1205) from Lyons was reading the Provençal translation of the Gospels. Struck by the call to itinerant preaching (Matt. 10), he took the requirements for discipleship of Jesus (in Matt. 10) literally: he gave away his possessions and with some followers (the 'Poor Men of Lyons') began to travel around preaching; he drew great crowds, because criticism of a church greedy for power and an ambitious and power-seeking clergy was already on everyone's lips. The Bishop of Lyons banned his preaching, because a layman was not entitled to proclaim the faith. Peter Waldo turned to the pope and appeared at the Third Lateran Council (1179). His credible ideal of poverty proved convincing and he was again allowed to preach, though he was to refrain from any instruction in the faith. Preaching poverty and repentance with no reference to faith very soon proved impossible; the Bishop of Lyons forbade him to preach a second time. Again Peter Waldo turned to the pope, but this time he met with a rebuff. A new pope had put an end to the politics of tolerance. Peter (like Luther later) appealed to his conscience, and the pope responded in 1184 with excommunication. Peter Waldo took the position that the gospel could be proclaimed only by people who lived by it, and continued in his ways. In so doing he had gone beyond the bounds of what appeared tolerable in a society divided into clerical and lay 'states': preaching and the administration of the sacraments were reserved for the clergy. Now the Waldensians' criticism of the church became more radical, and soon they had their own services, sacraments and preachers, including women; they refused to take the oath or engage in military service.

The rift could no longer be healed. The Waldensians rapidly spread from southern France to northern Italy, northern Spain, Flanders, Germany and Bohemia. Now the pope called for new state legislation against heretics. From 1184, the emperor Frederick I Barbarossa threatened heretics with the imperial ban, and the French king followed suit – for understandable reasons: the southern French nobility were trying to remove themselves as far as possible from the royal centralism based on Paris and sympathized with the Waldensians and their criticism of the church.

In 1184 the Cathars were excommunicated along with

the Waldensians. The Cathars (= the pure) were a religious group which did not stem from Christianity; they had their roots in Manichaeism (Mani, who died in 277, was the founder of a Persian religion) and had moved from the Black Sea to settle in the Balkans. There they organized as Bogomils (= friends of God) and disseminated their dualistic doctrine of the God of light and the God of darkness, which was close to Gnosticism and strictly ascetic, through upper Italy to southern France. Here they were called Cathars or Albigensians – after their stronghold, Albi, in Piedmont. Their ideal of poverty and criticism of the church allied them to the Christian Waldensians, and that was enough for the two movements to be lumped together by the church and state authorities. Roman emperors before Constantine had already persecuted the Manichaeans, so the use of state force against them seemed justified.

For a long time the movements were protected by the aristocracy of Southern France, so that they could develop freely in the region. Finally, in alliance with Rome, the French kings resolved on military action: for twenty years (from 1209 to 1229), the Albigensian wars were waged with the utmost cruelty; the Albigensians were virtually exterminated and the Waldensians decimated and expelled. The flourishing Provençal culture was destroyed, large strips of land were depopulated, and the south of France generally was won back for the French kings (who confiscated the estates of the rebellious nobility) and Roman Catholicism.

But the escalation of violence had only just begun. Louis IX of France and Emperor Frederick II punished heresy with the death penalty; three years after the end of the war (in 1232), the Inquisition was created as a permanent papal institution for persecuting heretics, and the Dominicans, a mendicant (= begging) and preaching order founded in 1216, were appointed to implement it. Denunciation, torture and burning were their way of dealing with outsiders who in the three centuries up to the Reformation were putting in question the increasingly fragile identity of the 'Christian West'. One horrific climax to this inhuman terror was the role of the Spanish Inquisition in the expulsion and extermination of Jews and Muslims after the reconquest of Spain from the Arabs. Another was the bloody role of the Inquisition in the Central European witch-craze, to which hundreds of thousands of women fell victim. In this connection an irrational fear of the end of the mediaeval order distorted the humane qualities of Christianity almost beyond recognition.

The Waldensians survived underground in small groups, and those of them who had been exiled provided the impetus for the rebellion of the Hussites and Bohemian Brethren in the fifteenth century. It was only with the unification of Italy after 1848 that the Waldensians were granted their civil rights. Today they form the small indigenous Protestant church of Italy.

● Another movement dedicated to poverty had quite a different destiny. It was begun by Francis of Assisi (Francesco Bernadone, who died in 1226 and was beatified as early as 1228). He was the son of a rich merchant, led a loose life and took part in military campaigns in his region. Various events conspired to make him bid farewell to his previous life. The climax came in the famous scene from 1206: Francis rejected his inheritance, stripped off his clothes, threw them at his father's feet and hid under the cloak of the bishop. From then on Francis wore the garb of a penitent, tended the sick and withdrew to the life of a hermit. In 1209, as with Peter Waldo, it is said to have been the gospel of the sending out of the disciples which finally led him to the way of poverty and itinerant preaching. He gathered some like-minded friends, and a year later had his penitential movement approved in Rome by the pope.

Perhaps he was in Rome once again in 1215 for the First Lateran Council. From this point on, his movement spread rapidly. He himself wanted to go to Morocco (though he only got as far as Spain) and to Syria (though he only got as far as Dalmatia) to convert the Muslims. In fact he did get as far as Egypt in 1219, and there he even preached before Sultan Melek-el-Kamel.

However, all this was only an adventurous prelude. Almost against his will, in 1223 he had given his movement a rule which constituted it as a mendicant order and secured it church recognition. Under the leadership of brother Elias it soon spread all over Western Europe. Francis himself increasingly withdrew into the hill country of Umbria. A few days before his death in 1226 he dictated his testament – a radical call to poverty which was to split the order soon after his death: the uncompromising 'spirituals' fought against the laxer 'conventuals', and after vigorous controversy the Franciscan order split into several branches. The fate of the Franciscans is remarkable in several respects. Unlike Peter Waldo, Francis of Assisi, who took Jesus' call to discipleship literally, did not aim at reform of the institutional church; even the order was the work of his friend and successor. All his life a layman, Francis firmly refused to cross the line which marked off the competence of the clergy. His preaching was not a criticism of the clergy or the church but a call to individual listeners to reflect and be converted. Here Francis was very much in line with the prevalent movements dedicated to poverty, but remained politically innocuous, and his movement could be integrated as an instrument of church reform. Moreover, new social conditions, particularly the increasing significance of the cities, required new pastoral methods, for which the mendicant orders (Franciscans, Dominicans, etc.) proved particularly useful. They were flexible and could settle anywhere, and thus were superior to the old orders

(Benedictines, etc.) which were settled in monastic bastions outside the cities.

Without doubt the Franciscan movement with its dedication to poverty achieved great successes; but it too proved that reform of the heart cannot be an alternative to reform of structures. Integration into a monopolistic religion as part of a 'division of labour' always also amounts to support for the *status quo*. The further development of the Western papal church has shown that the interweaving of political and ecclesiastical systems of rule and the way in which each supports the other did not allow far-reaching changes.

Waldensians and Franciscans are examples of numerous developments in mediaeval Christianity. The former could not anticipate the Reformation, which led to the next split in the church, because they were politically too weak; the latter could not make the Reformation superfluous because they were not interested in politics.

Reformation and Counter-Reformation

The changes which Christianity underwent between the early and the late Middle Ages are striking. Whereas in the early period Christianity represented liberation from superstition about mythical forces, witches and demons, at the end of this period it fell victim itself to a fatal proneness to superstition. All that was left of the early Christian refusal to serve in the army was the exemption of monks and clergy from military service (another aspect of the 'division of labour'); it had become a matter of course that heretics were to be fought with fire and sword and that war was to be waged on all unbelievers at the frontiers of the 'Holy Empire', especially in order to regain the Holy Land: hence the Crusades. The Crusades were for Christians 'holy wars' (of the kind of which Islam is often accused) and were waged against Wends and Russians, against Moors, Cathars and Hussites. Between 1096 and 1270 there were seven great crusades to Palestine, which had long been Arab/Muslim.

Under the leadership of the Franks or the Germans, with ideological and financial support from the popes, following the formula 'foreign policy to provide a distraction from domestic policy', a war was waged against the crisis in Christian political self-assurance which was becoming increasingly evident. Great religious leaders like Bernard of Clairvaux (1091–1153, one of the founders of the Cistercian order, a stricter form of the Benedictines) put themselves at the service of the ideology of the crusades and thought it quite appropriate for the armies gathering for the Near East to begin their 'battle' with the expulsion and murder of the Jews in Europe: at the beginning of the First Crusade (1096) the Jewish communities in the Rhineland (in Speyer, Worms, Mainz and Cologne) were exterminated. From then on Jews were persecuted in the same way as the heretics were combated by force of arms.

Uncertainty is also reflected in a change in the theological view of the world. The Dominicans, who have such a bad reputation as a result of their work in the Inquisition, also produced great theologians and mystics: Thomas Aquinas (1225–1274), the most significant theologian of the Middle Ages, systematized the theological knowledge of his time on the basis of the philosophy of Aristotle, whose writings had reached Europe through the Muslim Arabs and had been rediscovered. Meister Eckhart (1260–1327), another Dominican, also represented a new personal piety with his mystical immediacy to God, who dwells within every human being as a spark of the soul. He and other mystics of his time, male and female, sought a viable basis for their Christian faith in inwardnesss, since the traditional orders, including the church's orders, offered less and less certainty.

From faith to superstition

Charlemagne, *Capitulatio de partibus Saxoniae* (785)

'Anyone who, blinded after the manner of the heathen, believes someone to be a witch . . . will suffer death.'

Bishop Burchard of Worms, Penitentiary (c.1000)

'Anyone who, blinded by the devil and having again fallen victim to Satan, believes that witches ride by night . . . must perform a penance.'

Heinrich Institoris and Jakob Sprenger (Dominicans from Cologne, witch-hunters appointed by the pope), *Malleus Maleficarum* (The Hammer of the Witches, 1489)

The authors condemn 'the old view . . . that witchcraft is not real'; rather, 'It is the greatest heresy not to believe in witches.'

The crisis reached a first climax in the so-called great Western schism. From 1378 there were two popes, and from 1409 even three, each backed by rival church groups. The Council of Constance, which from 1414 met by Lake Constance, consequently declared itself to be above papal authority, deposed all three popes and elected a fourth. Lasting four years, this Council of Constance was the longest in history, but it did not really produce serious reforms. On the contrary, the Bohemian Reformer Jan Hus, having been guaranteed free passage to Constance, was condemned as a heretic there in 1415 and burnt. In subsequent centuries, further councils sitting in Basel, Ferrara, Florence and Rome attempted church reform and failed.

This was the world into which Martin Luther was born in 1483, in Eisleben in Thuringia. Against the background of growing social and political conflicts (the decline of the nobility, exploitation of the peasantry, the growing power of the local rulers), a church of rich prelates and poor priests attempted to assert itself, whereas the educated were discovering the humanistic values of antiquity, the pious were withdrawing into mystic circles, and ordinary people were being abandoned to superstition.

One last attempt, the Fifth Lateran Council, failed, and in March 1517 it was dissolved inconclusively. A few months later, on 31 October of the same year, with his Ninety-Five Theses Martin Luther kindled the sparks which were to begin the Reformation.

From Luther's Ninety-Five Theses of 1517

27. They preach only human doctrines who say that as soon as the money clinks into the money chest, the soul flies out of purgatory.

32. Those who believe that they can be certain of their salvation because they have indulgence letters will be eternally damned, together with their teachers.

43. Christians are to be taught that he who gives to the poor or lends to the needy does a better deed than he who buys indulgences.

The occasion was the growing trade in indulgences. Smart preachers announced that punishment for sins could be remitted for money and prayer. When Pope Leo X had difficulties in financing the building of the new cathedral of St Peter's, in 1517 he drafted an indulgence, of which half the proceeds were to go to him and the other half to the Archbishop of Mainz, who was in debt to the banking house of the Fuggers. Luther's Ninety-Five Theses against the indulgence, composed in Latin (and probably never nailed to the door of the Schlosskirche in Wittenberg, but sent to friends), was soon translated and distributed throughout Germany.

But things did not stop there. The Roman response to the Ninety-Five Theses was a process against Luther for heresy (1518); he was threatened with excommunication (1520) and then in fact excommunicated (1521). Luther responded with his first great programmatic works. He was able to, because Frederick the Wise, Elector of Saxony, refused to surrender him to the authorities; when Luther did not recant his works at the Diet of Worms in 1521, the imperial ban was pronounced on him, but Frederick arranged a friendly ambush on the return journey and had Luther brought to safety in the Wartburg. There he began on his translation of the New Testament, which was to become for the German language what the King James Version became for English.

Behind this political saga lies the dramatic loss of authority by the universal mediaeval powers of emperor and pope; and on the other hand a theology which for the first time since Constantine successfully questioned the role of Christianity as an ideological link between the political and the social order. For Luther, membership of the Roman church was no longer necessary for salvation; he relativized the clerical church by emphasizing the priesthood of all believers – and he did so by replacing the claim of the Roman hierarchy and its magisterium, which had lost credibility, with the sole authority of Holy Scripture.

This created the possibility of a new orientation which could also legitimate political emancipation from the unpopular centralists, the emperor and the pope, and it became possible to make inroads into the clerical structure (e.g. priests could marry).

Luther himself could not foresee all this in the first years of the Reformation movement, and even when half Europe had joined the Reformation, it was by no means his intention to form a new church or confession. For its success, his movement certainly needed the political background which Peter Waldo and Jan Hus had still lacked, but without Luther's personal 'conversion experience', which gave him considerable credibility, the success would not have been so great.

This conversion experience (Luther first set it down in writing in 1545, a year before his death) must have taken place in the years between 1514 and 1517. It had been preceded by a particularly strict life as an Augustinian monk. In his study in the tower of the monastery in Wittenberg the desperate Luther, who was overtaxing himself in self-discipline, was struck by the insight that no effort, however strenuous, can free a person from imperfection (sin) and finitude (death). A passage from Paul's Letter to the Romans, 'The just shall live by faith' (1.17), was the key, and for Luther and the Reformation that meant that only faith in the unconditional grace of God justifies human beings, and moral effort and good works cannot contribute anything to this. This doctrine of justification became the heart of the Reformation confession.

The principles of the Lutheran Reformation

sola gratia: *Only the grace* of God can justify a person and bring salvation.

sola fide: *Only faith* can be the human answer to God's offer of salvation; efforts towards good works are not the condition ('justification by works') but a consequence of faith.

sola scriptura: *Only Holy Scripture*, and neither tradition nor magisterium, is the criterion for true Christian faith.

Liberation from the tutelage of Rome and the emperor, the revaluation of the individual believer, and the Christian legitimation of political resistance liberated a revolutionary impulse to do away with social abuses. The peasants attempted to revolt, but Luther distanced himself from them; the Protestant leaders put a bloody end to the unrest, and became the real heads of their state churches. In this way at a regional level the churches were once again tamed politically. Nevertheless, from the beginning, the right of each individual believer to interpret the Bible inevitably meant that the churches of the Reformation would not only take many forms but also split apart.

In Zurich and Geneva Ulrich Zwingli (1484–1531) and Jean Calvin (1509–1564) developed other variants of the Reformation, which clashed with Luther's theology. It was only in the middle of the century that the Roman church had pulled itself together sufficiently to inaugurate its own reform at the Council of Trent (1545–1563), the 'Counter-Reformation' or the 'Catholic reform'. This council, in which the Protestants did not take part, could not now remedy the split in the church. The Counter-Reformation was increasingly implemented by force in the countries with Catholic rulers; for centuries it was impossible for the Roman Catholic church and the Protestant churches to come to any agreement and they forced each other into a pernicious polarization. What was right for one church was not approved of by the other, and vice versa, so that on both sides there were complementary losses of traditions and one-sidednesses which have lasted down to the present day.

In the Reformation, the internal differentiation within the mediaeval monopolistic church, its collapse into different states of life and the way in which it dealt with reformers led to an open break between the unitary thought of Rome and a Europe which was becoming increasingly aware of its regional and spiritual pluralism. This split is harder to overcome than the old dispute between Rome and Orthodoxy.

8

The Nineteenth Century

If two religious groups appeal to the same origin and make rival claims to absoluteness, then they will damage themselves: the result of the irreconcilable opposition between Catholic and Protestants in Europe was that many religious people left both churches.

Church, religion and ideology: a division

The present form of Western Christianity is essentially the result of the developments and conflicts of the nineteenth century. The division of the Western European church through the Reformation and the Counter-Reformation first led to bloody wars of religion (including the Huguenot wars in France between 1562 and 1598 and the Thirty Years' War in Germany between 1618 and 1648) in which whole areas of Europe were depopulated, and then to a pact between the different Christian confessions with their rival claims to absoluteness. Politics, first of all closely interwoven with religious interests, gradually sought an ideological platform above a confessional dispute which was beyond resolution. Since the divided Christian faith could no longer offer a spiritual foundation for peaceful co-existence, reason was regarded as the new point of reference. The 'age of the Enlightenment' was meant to bring emancipation from myths and bans on thinking. The French Revolution (1789) made reason itself a mythical ideology, and in Italy and Austria Catholic princes – in a tradition which had existed since Constantine – intervened in church life in the spirit of the Enlightenment (contrary to the will of the pope, the emperor Joseph II pushed through the abolition of 'unreasonable' orders, i.e. contemplative orders with no social involvement).

However, both approaches had similar consequences: despite all the privileges which still remained to it, the Roman Catholic church had to be one religion among others – whether through a royal patent of tolerance for Protestants and Jews (Joseph II, 1781), or through revolutionary declarations of religious freedom (point 10 of the 1789 Declaration on Human Rights). Resistance to a role to which it had not been accustomed for 1500 years continued in the Roman Catholic church down to the twentieth century. The Protestant churches were divided in their reactions: accustomed from the beginning to being split into various trends, for them the nineteenth century was the age of splintering into numerous movements, groups and confessions which ranged from extreme liberalism to a rigid biblical fundamentalism.

Now there was no longer the one Christianity as the monopolistic religion of society. Not only did the dispute between Christianities set free those religious people who were not bound to a confession, but outside the churches a free-floating religious practice became socially possible and was tolerated. The result of this division was that the superstition and pious scurrilities which had been kept under control in the churches or on their periphery now took independent shape in religious sects and political ideologies. The situation for Western Christianity became increasingly like that before Constantine – but with the difference that the churches now believed that they had to hold on to rights which they had not had at all before Constantine, and the new religion outside the churches could often claim to derive from the Christian tradition. On the other hand, new arguments advanced by the critics of religion, from Feuerbach to Freud, increasingly put Christianity in question.

1870 proved a significant year. The new German empire, which excluded Catholic Austria, realized the dream of the Protestant empire which since the sixteenth century had been a vain one. The proclamation of King Wilhelm of Prussia as German emperor in Versailles was also a late political answer to three and a half centuries of Catholic predominance in Europe. In the same year the unification of Italy put an end to the church state and reduced papal power to spiritual claims. These claims were advanced in the same year at the First Vatican Council, which promulgated the dogma of papal infallibility and led to a new division (the Old Catholic Church came into being in 1871) and to a further sharp distancing from Protestants.

These developments increasingly made the churches seem socially irrelevant, and the close contact of Christianity with science and art which had lasted for centuries was lost. For a long time their preoccupation with themselves made the churches blind to the most pressing question of the time, the wretched state of the working class. Certainly there were numerous individual political initiatives, and aid was organized by Christians, but the great political scheme for a new order in society came without Christianity and contrary to it. Because of its rejection of religion, Marxism (the Communist Manifesto of 1848) was no conversation partner for the churches. Alternative Christian schemes (e.g. the first social encyclical of Pope Leo XIII in 1891) in which the individual initiatives of bold pioneers were brought together and implemented as policies came into being only at a late stage. Although Christianity as a whole was already on the defensive, where the confessions had any political influence they continued with their wars of religion as cultural battles – among one another and against the new 'confession' of anticlericalism, whose advocates presented themselves in the guise of warriors of faith. Like scientists and artists before them, now intellectuals and workers also turned their backs on the churches.

On the threshold of the twentieth century, what was left was a bourgeois, rural church society which still attached importance to the alliance between throne and altar, but was already slowly beginning to fall apart.

Colonialism and mission

One could start this subject with the Crusades, but at the latest it begins with the discovery of America. From the beginning, European imperialism used Christianity to legitimate its claims to rule. The Spanish conquerors really believed, or pretended to believe, that they were pleasing God in their subjection of the original population of America, whereas in reality they were in search of gold and a cheap labour force. Belief in witches and the devil at the beginning of modern times helped: non-Christian religions and non-Christian cultures were regarded as the work of Satan which had to be exterminated with every possible means, including bloody violence.

Certainly voices were raised against this. The Spanish Dominican Bartolomé de las Casas (1474–1566) called for respect for the human rights of the Indians, but his famous appearance before the emperor Charles V in 1551 could not contribute towards making the emperor's laws which favoured the Indians effective. From 1608 in Paraguay the Jesuits established a model state with Indian self-government, but they were driven out with church support in the middle of the century of the Enlightenment (1767). Their heirs, the Franciscans, had little regard for indigenous culture; they had already joined forces with the Dominicans between 1601 and 1607 in suppressing the Jesuit mission in

China in which, for the first time in more recent history, a successful attempt had been made to inculturate Christianity in a highly-developed non-European civilization. The slavers did their work in Africa for a long time with the backing or tolerance of Christians: so Latin America, Asia and Africa came to know Christianity predominantly as an ideology of European expansion.

The nineteenth century brought a new wave of European colonialism to which now the Islamic countries of North Africa and the Middle East fell victim. Napoleon's landing in Egypt in 1798 was the first step towards establishing the interests of European hegemony on the eastern and southern shores of the Mediterranean. Sensing the triumph of enlightened reason, Europeans saw the whole world as subject to them and felt justified in dominating it. This European domination was certainly no longer a Christian one; however, we cannot overlook the fact that throughout the nineteenth century all the Christian churches, both Catholic and Protestant, used the protection of colonialism to engage in a Europeanizing mission in every corner of the earth. And the missionaries were welcomed by the colonial powers because they gave some cultural embellishment to the business of political domination and economic exploitation. So we can understand how from the perspective of those being colonized Christians were often regarded as traitors to their countries, and in rebellions and outbreaks of xenophobia (like the Boxer rebellion in China in 1900) became the victims of the new nationalisms. Down to the middle of this century a new kind of martyr from the 'Christian colonies' served to provide a romantic transfiguration of missionary activity: the personal testimony of these martyrs was a strange mixture, since at the same time they had become the victims of Europeanizing alienation.

Nevertheless, in this connection too one of the age-old tensions in Christianity was at work: a new form of political subversion of the legitimation of power. Christianity also became the religion of the black American slaves and the Indios who had been deprived of their rights; from it they derived that deep trust in God which helped them to survive, and which we still admire in their spirituals. That strand of tradition which reaches from the poverty of the first itinerant preachers through the poverty movements of the Middle Ages to the immense charitable efforts made by the Christian churches today was capable of giving credibility to Christianity in the eyes of the oppressed. Hence, despite colonial rule, South America is a Christian continent, and large parts of Africa have been Christianized, even in places where Islam could not be overcome.

The population explosion in the Third World also contributed towards shifting the focus of Christianity. In the middle of this century the number of Christians in the southern hemisphere passed that of the Christians in the countries of Europe and North America. Between 1930 and 1965 the world population increased by 58.7%, but the increase was only 25% in Europe, as compared with 63% in Asia, 89% in Africa, and even 125% in Latin America. Caught up in this development, the growth of the number of Christians was also very different: whereas in 1900 85% of all Christians still lived in Europe and North America, in the year 2000 the proportion will be only 40%.

Such a shift cannot fail to have an effect. Indigenous theologies are developing everywhere, and the split between an upper-class church thinking in European terms and the concern with inculturation in a grass-roots church of the poor is one of the permanent conflicts of the present, epecially in Latin America.

The focal point of the development of Christianity in the first millennium lay in the east of Europe and the eastern Mediterranean. In the second millennium the scene of the controversies of this religion was the West.

It could be that the third millennium of Christianity will be dominated by a Christianity of the Third World, since Western Christianity has exhausted itself and got stuck in so many historical controversies.

The East: the burden and splendour of tradition

The Christianity of the East, which had dominated antiquity, increasingly disappeared from the perspective of Western church history after the split with Rome in 1054. However, that is not just a matter of perspective. In fact the territories of the Eastern church, the old patriarchates of Antioch, Alexandria and Jerusalem, had already been overrun by the expansion of Islam from the seventh century on; they were tolerated under Islamic rule, but did not and could not have any significance for church politics. Constantinople, the second Rome, which for a long time called itself Byzantium, lost territory after territory under pressure from the Arabs and the Slavs, was for a while stripped of power by the West when Venice used the Crusades to develop its economic basis in the eastern Mediterranean, and finally in 1453 fell into the hands of the Ottomans.

The patriarch of Constantinople, who resides in Turkish Istanbul, still has a primacy of honour among the Orthodox churches. But as early as 1589 the Russian church made itself independent, seeing the Czars as the successors to the Byzantine emperors, and declaring Moscow to be the third Rome. Aware of this, the Czars again abolished the position of patriarch, from 1721 to 1917 ruling the Russian church in their own names and with the help of a clerical assembly (the 'Holy Synod'). There has again been a patriarch in Russia since the October Revolution of 1917.

The gradual decline of the Ottoman empire over two centuries after the siege of Vienna by the Turks in 1683 led the new Slavonic nation states belatedly to follow the

Russian example: church independence (autocephaly) was declared by the Serbs in 1830, the Greeks in 1833, the Roumanians in 1856 and the Bulgarians in 1870, and they organized themselves under their own patriarchs or archbishops.

After the schism of 1054, repeated attempts were made to restore unity between the Eastern and the Western churches (in 1274 the Second Council of Lyons; in 1439 the union of Ferrara/Florence); however, the agreements between the heads of churches were paper treaties. A last agreement in 1452 promised success, but it was overtaken a few months later by the Ottoman conquest of Byzantium. The attempts at union made since then have always affected only small parts of the Orthodox church, which had to recognize papal authority for political reasons, and as a consequence were allowed to retain their rites and church languages (Catholic churches in the East, Uniate churches). The Ukrainians, Roumanians, Slovaks and others who are united with Rome regard themselves as bridges to Orthodoxy, but at the same time are a hindrance to ecumenical dialogue between the Eastern and the Western churches because from an Eastern perspective they are renegades and in no way a model for future church unity. And while in 1965 Pope Paul VI and Patriarch Athenagoras rescinded the reciprocal anathemas of 1054, virtually no practical conclusions have been drawn from this.

The persecution of the Orthodox churches, along with distorted variants of the old state church, have led to a further climax in our century: the church of Russia has had to live under state atheism with a Communist stamp for seventy years, as for forty years have the Orthodox churches of Eastern Europe (along with the Uniate churches). Since the Caesaropapism of the beginnings and its suppression by Islam, up to and including this last experience, the Christianity of the East has found different values from those of the West to be important. Freedom, dialectic, justification, everything deriving from the philosophical thought of both Rome and its opponents which still provides material for endless controversies, had little significance in the East. Here the tradition of the Greek church fathers was and is continued; here icons are venerated as the archetype of the Holy; here the sung liturgy is the vehicle for both popular piety and a theology which is expounded poetically.

There are also doctrinal disputes in Orthodoxy, but with few exceptions they have not taken on the significance that they still have in Western Christianity. Meditation and mysticism are more important, perhaps also because all bishops have been monks (they alone are obligated to celibacy), whereas the married deacons and priests have remained close to life and have maintained links with the people. In Orthodoxy there was no new generally binding council after the seven ecumenical councils. Much may seem old-fashioned and retarded to Western eyes, but this was the only way in which the church could survive. The fact that in the meantime Western civilization (with all its un-Christian features) has become the world civilization and is also making an impact in Orthodox countries will be the next challenge for Eastern Christianity.

The nineteenth century shows a defensive Christianity behind barricades, detaching itself from world developments, and at the same time a collection of new world-views which regard this development as the better religion. This century distorts our view of Christianity because it makes historically conditioned controversies appear as fundamental conflicts. Only today, after much jockeying for position, is it again becoming clearer what this religion is really about.

9

Like Sand on the Seashore

There has probably never been such a thing as Christianity (in the singular). The controversies in the history of this religion have constantly given rise to new churches and confessions which have emerged from a coalition of dissidents from the old ones. So it is possible to construct a 'genealogy' of Christian groups which branch out increasingly as we approach the present day.

Churches, free churches and sects

The following survey can only be a rough division and cannot explain the difference between types of faith. Some of these derive from the situations in which churches were formed, situations which have already been described in the historical chapters of this book. The dates are meant to provide some basic guidelines and refer either to the year in which churches came into being (split off) and/or were recognized, or the year of the event which proved a catalyst or (where there are several dates) the year of re-establishment.

In 1970, with around one billion believers, Christianity made up 30% of the population of the world. Although the number of Christians is increasing, the proportion of the population that they represent is declining, and after 2000 they will form only 25%.

1. The Churches of the East

The churches formed from the earliest splits

The Arian churches (from after 325 until the seventh century)
The Apostolic Church of the East (Nestorians), 424/431

The Council of Nicaea in 325 condemned Arius, but the Arian variant of Christianity nevertheless dominated the Germanic realms of the migrations for a long time. In the next century, Nestorius was condemned at the Council of Ephesus in 431. The Nestorian Church, also the 'East Syrian Church', formerly in Persia with missions to China, now exists in Iraq and Iran, in Syria and in the United States, with over 150,000 members.

The ancient Eastern churches

Armenian Apostolic Church, 451 (already a Christian state church in 374)
Coptic Orthodox Church, 451 in Egypt
Syrian Orthodox Church (also 'West Syrian Church' or 'Jacobites'), organized in 451/543
Orthodox Church of India, after 451 primarily East Syrian (Nestorian, see above)/ in 1655 West Syrian in opposition to the colonialist supervision from Rome
Ethiopian Orthodox church, since 550 a state church/ only dependent on the Coptic Church in 1959

Monophysitism was condemned at the Council of Chalcedon in 451. However, five churches did not recognize the condemnation and played no part in later councils. Today these churches number more than 30 million believers, almost half of them in Ethiopia.

The Orthodox Churches (after 1054)

The four ancient patriarchates of Constantinople, Alexandria, Antioch and Jerusalem, and the church of Cyprus have existed since antiquity. The most important foundation of more modern times is the Russian Orthodox Church, first in Kiev, and then with the Patriarchate of Moscow (1589/ 1917).

It was only in the last century that Orthodoxy was further divided along nationalistic lines into autonomous churches, a process which continued up to the Second World War: the Patriarchate of Sofia (1782/1961), the Church of Greece (1850), the Church of Georgia (1917), the Patriarchate of Belgrade (1922), the Church of Czechoslovakia (1922), the Archdiocese of Finland (1922), the Church of Poland (1924), the Patriarchate of Bucharest (1925), the Church of Albania (1937).

The Orthodox churches are not separate confessions: their liturgical ceremonies and languages differ, but their faith is the same. They are more strongly linked with national interests than the Roman Catholic Church usually is; thus at present the Orthodox Church in the former republic of Yugoslavia is seeking independence and both the Serbian and Greek Orthodox Churches are attempting to prevent this. Since the split with Russia, there has been a similar controversy over a new independent Orthodox Church of the Ukraine which has not yet been recognized. Today the Orthodox churches number around 150 million members, almost half of them belonging to the Russian Orthodox Church.

The Old Believers (Starovery)

These derive from the most significant of a number of splits within Orthodoxy. In the great schism (Raskol) of 1653 they first opposed the liturgical reforms of Nikon, patriarch of Moscow, which were in a Greek direction, and subsequently became opponents of the state church (rejecting marriage, the swearing of oaths and military service); as a result they suffered harsh persecutions under the Czars. A moderate trend has been able to survive to the present day.

2. The Churches of the West

The Catholic churches (after 1054)

The Roman Catholic Church
The Catholic Eastern Churches

From early times the Bishop of Rome had occupied the fifth ancient patriarchate as patriarch of the West; as pope he claimed supremacy over the whole of Christianity. The present Roman Catholic Church is this church of the pope, and the largest of the Christian churches. Until this century its liturgical language was Latin; it is organized as a strictly hierarchical and monarchical church. It is the only Christian church which requires all its priests (and not just bishops, as in Orthodoxy) to be unmarried (celibate); like the churches of the East, the Old Catholics, the High Church Anglicans and some Lutheran churches in Scandinavia, it maintains the apostolic succession (i.e. every bishop and priest from the time of the apostles can be appointed to office only through consecration by another legitimate minister); in it the pope not only has a primacy of honour but also the competence to make the ultimate decision in all matters. Today, with 900 million members, the Roman Catholic Church comprises more than half of all Christians.

The Uniate or Catholic Eastern churches broke their links with the Orthodox patriarchate after 1054, and submitted to the Roman pope. The main reasons for this were the changes to the frontiers between the Western and Eastern spheres of influence and the result of missionary work in the wake of Western European colonial policy. So there are Uniates from almost all the Eastern churches (e.g. Armenian Uniates, 1198–1375, 1740; Ruthenian Uniates [Ukrainians], 1595/9; Ethiopian and Coptic Uniates; Serbian, Syrian, Roumanian, Bulgarian, Greek and Russian Uniates). The Uniates share the belief of Roman Catholics, but have their traditional rites, their old liturgical languages and their own canon law; their priests are usually married, and their bishops are elected from an assembly of clergy and confirmed by the pope. Today the Catholic Eastern churches have around 10 million members.

The Old Catholics

Resistance to the dogma of papal infallibility (at the First Vatican Council, 1870) led to the foundation in Germany in 1871 of an Old Catholic Church, which based its confession on the faith of the undivided church of the first millennium. In 1875, communities in Switzerland which did not recognize the Roman dogma combined to form the Christian Catholic Church. At a later date, Polish National Catholic Churches were formed in Poland and the USA. Today the Old Catholic churches, which are united by the Union of Utrecht (1889), have around 500,000 members.

3. The Pre-Reformation churches

Waldensians, 1215
Hussites, 1414
Bohemian Brethren, 1467

The pioneers of reform in the later Middle Ages who were not integrated into the mainstream church but were sometimes harshly persecuted are seen in retrospect as forerunners of the Reformation, by which they were in turn strongly influenced.

The Waldensians are active today above all in Piedmont, southern Italy, Sicily and South America (Uruguay), with around 50,000 members.

Some of the Hussites contented themselves with the demand of communion from the chalice for the laity (the term used for this is 'Utraquists', i.e. those calling for communion in two kinds, both bread and wine); others of them, under the influence of the Waldensians, were more sharply critical of the Roman church. A new Hussite church was founded as a Czech national church after the First World War.

The radical heritage of the Hussites lived on in the Bohemian Moravian Brethren (1467), who separated from the Utraquists as early as 1467 and refused to take oaths or do military service. They were refounded in the eighteenth century: Count Zinzendorf (1700–1760) took up their spirituality in the Herrnhut Community of Brethren, and through this they have been a stimulus for revival movements down to the present day. The present-day Unity of Brethren numbers about 400,000 members on four continents.

4. The Churches of the Reformation (after 1517)

The Lutheran Churches

The Reformation movement which began with Martin Luther was not only opposed to the Roman church but also remained separate from the left-wing political radicals involved in the Peasants' War and from the Swiss Reformers Zwingli and Calvin (1509–1564). Its confessional basis is the Augsburg Confession of 1530 (composed by Luther's closest fellow-worker, Philip Melanchton, for the Reichstag in Augsburg). The churches of Luther's Reformation spread above all in Germany and northern Europe and are organized into state churches. This was because of the special political significance of the local rulers for the Reformation (the churches are still state churches in Scandinavia). Since 1947 these churches have come together in the Lutheran World Federation, and with 140 churches and about 70 million members they form the largest block of Christian churches after Rome and Orthodoxy.

The Reformed Churches

Zwinglians, 1536/1566
Calvinists, 1537
Huguenots, 1559

In Switzerland, which had been independent of the German empire since 1499, the Reformation began independently of Martin Luther. Ulrich Zwingli (1484–1531) started it in Zurich and Jean Calvin, who was younger (1509–1564), did so in Geneva (cf. p.64). A dispute over the significance of the Lord's Supper, in which Zwingli emphasized more the remembrance of Jesus than his real presence in bread and wine, led to a separate development of the Reformed churches (First Helvetic Confession, 1536). Whereas many Lutheran churches have the episcopate, the Reformed churches in principle have a democratic synodical constitution. So unlike the episcopal churches (those with bishops), they often term themselves 'presbyterian', because the elected governing body composed of clergy and laity is called the 'presbytery'. Their confessional basis is the gospel, and in addition some Reformed churches have the Second Helvetic Confession composed by Heinrich Bullinger (1504–1575), Zwingli's successor, in 1566. From 1537 onwards, Calvin's Reformation established a strictly moralistic religious regime in Geneva under which deviants were proceeded against with methods characteristic of the Inquisition. The theory of Max Weber, the sociologist of religion, that there is a close connection between the Calvinist attitude and the spread of capitalism is not to be dismissed out of hand. The Reformed church spread principally in Switzerland, France, the Netherlands, England and the USA. The Huguenots (a term which possibly derives from the French pronunciation of the German word *Eidgenossen*, confederates) had their first national synod in Paris. Up to the French Revolution they often suffered bloody persecution; even now they are the small, active core of French Protestantism.

A new Reformed World Alliance was formed in 1970 from a Reformed World Alliance of 1875 and a Congregationalist World Alliance of 1879; today it numbers between 40 and 60 million members (the figures fluctuate).

United churches

Over the past century a complicated network of bilateral negotiations has brought together many of the churches of divided Protestantism, i.e. in eucharistic fellowship. Only in the present day has an agreement (the Leuenberg Concord of 1973) made a new beginning towards settling the sixteenth-century dispute over the Lord's Supper.

The Anglican Church, 1534

Initially, the Anglican Church was not a Reformation church; it owes its origin to the break between King Henry VIII of England and the pope, who wanted to refuse him permission to divorce and remarry. But tendencies towards the independence of the Church of England are older. Already in the *Magna carta libertatum* of 1215 we find the statement '*Ecclesia Anglicana sit libera*' ('Let the English church be free'), against which the then pope, Innocent III, protested vigorously. When 300 years later King Henry VIII could not get Rome to annul his first marriage (which had produced no children), this personal problem was compounded with the British desire for autonomy; the Reformation in continental Europe was also encouragement for action.

In 1534 the English parliament declared the king supreme head of the Church of England. It was only with the 1549 Book of Common Prayer and the Forty-Two Articles (which took over the Lutheran doctrine of justification and the Calvinistic doctrine of the Lord's Supper) that the Church of England joined the Reformation theologically and liturgically. An attempt at re-Catholicization during the reign of Mary (1553–1558) remained an episode. When in 1601 Ireland became British, but stayed Catholic, a political and confessional hostility began which to the present day has led to bitter conflicts.

At a very early stage not only the Catholics, but also Reformed Christians, were opposed to the Anglican state church. The Puritans practised a strict English variant of Calvinism, from the middle of the sixteenth century turning against the sensuality of the Elizabethan era. From 1583 a 'High Commission' of the Anglican church was behind the persecution of 'Noncomformists' and dissenters. A century of revolutions and civil war on British soil ended in 1688 with the 'Glorious Revolution' and the Acts of Tolerance of 1689 (though these did not apply to Catholics).

The Puritans were forced to emigrate to America in a series of waves. But from the foundation of the first English colony in North America (Virginia 1582) there was also an Anglican mission in the New World. The Anglican church increasingly developed into three main streams: the High Church is closest to the Catholics in hierarchy and liturgy; the Low Church nowadays is evangelical and closest to the Puritan understanding of faith; the Broad Church represents a liberal Christianity. These variants and the opposition between the established Church of England and Puritanism have left their stamp on British and North American religion down to the present day.

The Anglican church today numbers 68 million members, above all in the area of the former British colonies and the Commonwealth; barely half of them live in Europe.

The Anglo-American Protestants

Here I shall mention the two dominant currents, which split into numerous individual churches (see also below, under 'Free Churches').

Presbyterians, 1647

The arrival of the Calvinist Reformation in the British Isles created opposition to the hierarchical Anglican state church above all in Scotland. The Scottish Reformer John Knox (1505–1572), a disciple of Calvin, established a democratic church order without bishops which was congenial to the Scottish national consciousness as it confronted English claims to power. On the basis of the Westminster Confession of 1647 Presbyterianism spread from Scotland and Ireland to America and Australia; today Presbyterians number between 5 and 6 million.

Congregationalists, 1582/1832

Convinced that the Church of England could not be renewed from within, in 1582 Robert Brown established an independent community in Norwich (they were known as 'Independents'), thus creating an alternative to the dominant state church, which reacted with persecution and expulsion. A group of emigrants who had settled in Leiden, in Holland, set sail for America in 1620 in their ship the Mayflower (they are known as the Pilgrim Fathers), and founded the city of Plymouth. From that beginning Congregationalism, with the principle 'a church without a bishop and a state without a king', became the dominant church system in North American Protestantism. In England there has only been a union of Congregational communities since 1832. Congregationalists have no church structures beyond the individual community; here they also differ from the Presbyterians. Today it is thought that there are around four million Congregationalists, but their number is probably greater, because most of them are involved in unions with other churches.

5. The Free Churches

Mennonites, 1540
Baptists, 1609
Quakers, 1647
Methodists, 1738
Salvation Army, 1865
Pentecostal churches, since 1900

Individual groups of Reformation Christians have parted company with the great confessions for various reasons: through a rejection of state supervision, in protest against the liberal theology of nineteenth century, or in the wake of new revivalist movements. The Free Churches stand in the tradition of the sixteenth-century Anabaptist movement. They have in common an emphasis on believers' baptism, i.e. usually adult baptism, and the requirement of personal conversion. One cannot be 'born into' a free church.

The Mennonites (named after the Friesian priest Menno Simons, 1495–1561) form the earliest Anabaptist church still extant (since 1540). They preach non-violence, are among the earliest advocates of the idea of tolerance, and in 1688 provided the first impetus towards the abolition of slavery at a synod in Germantown, in America. Today they number around 600,000 worldwide.

The Baptists are by far the largest of these churches. John Smyth founded the first community in Amsterdam in 1609 with English emigrants. They too are characterized by non-violence and conscientious objection to military service. Worldwide (excluding children and friends), there are 32 million Baptists, the overwhelming majority of them in North America. Every other black person in the USA is a Baptist. 600,000 Baptists live in the lands of the former USSR, where until the collapse of Communism they were exposed to severe persecution.

The Quakers (more accurately 'The Religious Society of Friends') represent a Christianity without dogma and sacraments. Their name was originally a derisive nickname. Their founder, George Fox, 1624–1691, first called his visionary, enthusiastic group 'Children of the Light' or 'Friends of the Truth', later 'Society of Friends'. William Penn (1644–1718), the founder of Pennsylvania and one of the most significant Quaker figures, provided for complete freedom of religion, the abolition of the military and no oath-taking or church marriage in his state. Non-violence, the fight against slavery, deep commitment to social justice, to refugees and the starving (after the Second World War, in the Vietnam War, etc.), have been characteristics of their history from the beginning to the present day. Of the 200,000 Quakers, 120,000 live in North America.

Methodism was initially a reform movement within the Church of England. It began with a personal religious experience of the Anglican priest John Wesley (1703–1791) in 1738, comparable to Luther's experience in the tower. This led him to carry on unresting missionary activity as a preacher on horseback through England, Scotland and Ireland. In 1784 Wesley ordained the first preachers for North America, where the Methodist movement spread like wildfire. The Methodists have never understood themselves as a confession over against other confessions and today are among the most committed advocates of church co-operation in the ecumenical movement. At present there are 20 million Methodists worldwide (not counting children and friends). The Methodist minister William Booth (1829–1912) and his wife Catherine began mission and social work in London's East End in 1865. In 1878 they gave their work a strict military organization; today the Salvation Army works in 100 countries with four million members: it shows enormous dedication to the poor, the hungry, refugees, and so on; here help and moral support go hand in hand.

Like the Methodists, the Pentecostal churches are not a confession over against other confessions. However, under the impact of the ecstatic phenomena which marked their beginnings, they show little readiness for dialogue with other churches. Since the beginning of this century American revivalist movements with a fundamentalist character have understood their conversion experiences as 'baptism with the Spirit'. The different Pentecostal churches – membership worldwide is estimated at 30 million – are gaining followers above all in the Third World, where they are developing a personally stimulating but at the same time socially and politically reassuring spirituality.

6. North American Christianity

In North America, the Protestants were the Christians who largely shaped society: in the USA they form 46% of the population, as opposed to 3.6% Anglicans and 30% Catholics; in Canada, however, Catholics form 46.6% of the population, as opposed to 29.6% Protestants and 10.5% Anglicans. North American Catholicism has been stamped by immigration from Ireland and therefore has to cope with conflicts with immigrants from other Catholic cultures (Poles and Italians).

From the beginning, several of the thirteen original colonies in North America were a refuge for those suffering religious persecution. The 'way West' mixed the confessions and led to 'denominationalism' as a typically American phenomenon: a number of independent churches formed within one and the same denomination, leading alternately to competition and co-operation. This is the basis for a new form of Christian tolerance and ecumenism, of which Anglicans and Catholics have also had to take account.

All the churches and free churches mentioned earlier, above all those of English and Scottish origin, are 'American', as too are the Pentecostal churches. In addition there are religious communities which have come into being in America itself; these represent variants of Christianity, but cannot simply be regarded as Christian churches. Their history begins in the second quarter of the nineteenth century with a wave of eschatological belief, a sense of living in the last days.

The farmer William Miller (1782–1849) calculated that Christ would return in 1843/44. After this expectation was disappointed and reinterpreted (Christ had come invisibly), in 1863 his adventist movement issued in the Community of the Seventh-Day Adventists, whose faith centres on the Ten Commandments, the sanctification of the sabbath and social service. Today this church numbers 4.5 million members in 186 countries.

Thirty years later, an Adventist splinter group inspired the Pittsburgh businesman Charles Taze Russell (1852–1916) to found the journal *Zion's Watch Tower* (1879). Along with this went a large-scale scriptural mission. Russell's community called itself 'International Bible Students', but since 1931 has been known as Jehovah's Witnesses. The end of the wicked world was first calculated as 1874 and most recently as 1975. On these dates a final apocalyptic battle would destroy everything, including even the Christian churches, with the exception of the righteous, namely Jehovah's Witnesses. A literal understanding of the Bible prohibits them from consuming blood or having blood transfusions; they are conscientious objectors to military service. Worldwide, they number more than three million adherents.

The Church of Jesus Christ of the Latter-Day Saints (Mormons) also derives from the apocalyptic era of the 1840s. From the age of fourteen the farmer's son Joseph Smith (1805–1844) had visions calling on him to restore the church. In 1830 he founded his church with its own hierarchy; in 1844 he was murdered in prison. To avoid persecution the Mormons then went out West, to territory where there were as yet no settlers, and founded Salt Lake City and the State of Utah. Alongside the Bible, the foundation of their faith is the Book of Mormon, which was revealed to Smith and according to which a saved American people emigrated from Israel to America centuries previously and then became extinct. The Mormons have a secret temple worship and retrospective baptism of the dead (resulting in an extensive system of genealogical research). Polygamy was practised between 1843 and 1896. The Mormons number more than six million members, half of them in the USA.

7. Sects

Sects can only be regarded as Christian groups with many qualifications. Many of them – in the same way as the Mormons, Jehovah's Witnesses and some Pentecostal churches – reject the creeds of the councils of the early church and refuse to collaborate with other Christian churches or have additional books of revelation outside the Bible. Most sects active today derive from American fundamentalism and expect an imminent end to the world. New radical

forms ('youth religions') have very few traces of Christianity; the danger they pose lies in their combination of a
business sense and an interest in power with a heedless
missionary zeal, at the same time (unlike the Christian
churches) avoiding any public discussion.

Ecumenism

The technical church term 'ecumenical' is often confused
with 'economical' – and with some justification, since
behind the two terms stands the Greek word for 'dwell',
'run a household' (= economy), but also 'inhabit', namely
the whole of the habitable earth. Thus in antiquity the
ecumene was the sphere of the Roman empire; now it means
the whole world. In the previous century, the conflict
between the universal claim of Christianity and its many
divisions was particularly evident when Christians of different confessions attempted to compete in mission in Africa
and Asia. From an insight into the degree to which
Christianity was thus continually compromising itself,
among the Protestant churches an ecumenical movement
developed which aroused in the various traditions an
awareness of the fundamental unity of Christianity. The
first interconfessional Bible societies had already come into
being around 1800. International 'missionary conferences'
took place in London in 1878 and 1888, and these were
followed by the 'World Missionary Conferences' of New
York (1900) and Edinburgh (1910).

From the Constitution of the World Council of Churches

*'The World Council of Churches is a fellowship of churches
which confess the Lord Jesus Christ in accordance with
Holy Scripture as God and Saviour and therefore seek to
fulfil their common calling to the glory of God the Father,
the Son and the Holy Spirit.'*

From then on a whole series of initiatives took place which in 1948 led to the formation of the World Council of Churches (WCC, with its headquarters in Geneva). 147 churches from 44 countries were represented at the Assembly in Amsterdam which marked its foundation. In 1961 the great Orthodox churches of Eastern Europe and the first Pentecostal churches joined the WCC. Today the WCC has over 300 member churches from 90 countries, with 400 million members. The Christian 'minimal requirement' is a recognition of the Bible as a book of revelation; belief in Jesus, the Christ and Son of God; and belief in God as Trinity.

The WCC does not understand itself as a superchurch, and membership of it does not imply any agreement with other churches. Nevertheless, the Roman Catholic Church does not belong to the WCC. For a long time, Roman Catholicism could conceive of unity and collaboration between Christians of different confessions only as a return to the papal church. It was the Second Vatican Council (1962–1965) which first recognized non-Roman Christian communities as churches. Since 1961, on the initiative of Pope John XXIII, the Roman Catholic Church has had observer status, and collaborates in commissions and committees.

Whereas the unity of Christianity was for a long time understood primarily as a combination of organizations, reducing the different traditions to the one prevailing at a particular time, nowadays Christians think in more democratic and federalist terms; for only if the mutual condemnations, the war between churches, comes to an end, will Christianity preserve its place among the world religions.

After a 2000-year history of splits, the ecumenical movement has led to the insight that the confession of the faith of the Bible and the early church binds all Christians together.

10

Christianity as a Way

One can study the theology of Christianity; one can put its history critically under a microscope; but none of this would have any significance had there not been people at all times who understood this religion as a help and an illumination in their personal life. Holy times in the church's year, holy signs in the liturgy, and a particular view of life are characteristic of Christianity, for all its splits.

Worship and sacraments

The great variety of forms in which Christian worship is celebrated in the different confessions and on different occasions can easily disguise the fact that this worship is always composed of the same few elements.

As worship always celebrates, recalls and represents the encounter of human beings with God and God with human beings, it takes place in a dialogical interplay. It begins with:

1. Confession of sin and prayer for forgiveness. The church word for this ('penance', 'penitence') denotes the insight that human beings live in a broken and damaged situation and therefore need God. The second step is:

2. Reading from the Bible (Old and New Testaments), which is understood as the Word of God, to the assembled community. Here memories and reports of experiences of salvation are set over against the need for salvation which has been acknowledged. In the sermon these readings are then explained and related to the present.

3. The confession of faith (creed) formulates the assent of the community to the 'word of God' in the form of a shared declaration. In the wording of the councils of Nicaea and Constantinople the text acknowledges the threefold nature of God (Trinity) as Father, Son and Holy Spirit, and above all the significance of the Son Jesus Christ in salvation history. In the early church, catechumens (those being prepared for baptism) could only attend worship thus far. Now follows the heart of Christian worship.

4. The Lord's Supper. This is a re-enactment of Jesus' last supper with his followers before his arrest and execution. According to the Gospel reports, at that time Jesus said that the bread was his body and the wine his blood, and asked those at table with him to repeat this celebration in remembrance of him. In the course of worship this is understood as the highest level of the presence of God after God's presence in the Word (see above), after the community has confessed its faith. The celebration of the eucharist comes to a climax in the eating of bread and drinking of wine (communion).

5. There follow praise, thanksgiving and intercession, in keeping with the dialogical course of worship, and particularly in keeping with this climax. However, such prayers, whether spoken or sung, also accompany all other parts of worship and form an essential part of every celebration.

These five elements are the basic ingredients of all Christian worship. Whereas the Orthodox, Roman, High Church Anglican and Old Catholic traditions attach supreme value to the Lord's Supper or eucharist (from the Greek word for thanksgiving), in the Protestant churches, and above all in the Reformed churches, the emphasis is more on the first three elements, above all on the reading and interpretation of the Bible. Roman Catholics call the whole service the 'mass' or 'eucharist'; Protestants talk of 'worship' and the Orthodox of 'liturgy'.

The most prominent prayer

The 'Our Father' is the normative and most important
Christian prayer text, which all churches and confessions
have in common. The Gospel according to Matthew
reports preaching by Jesus in Galilee in which he said:
'When you pray, do not heap up empty phrases as the
Gentiles do, for they think that they will be heard for their
many words' (Matt.6.7).

As an alternative to this, Jesus formulates a prayer with
seven petitions:

Our Father who art in heaven,
Hallowed be thy name.
Thy kingdom come,
Thy will be done,
On earth as it is in heaven.
Give us this day our daily bread;
And forgive us our debts,
As we also have forgiven our debtors.
and lead us not into temptation,
But deliver us from evil.

A religion which believes in the incarnation of God has a
special connection with the tension between the visible and
the invisible. Similar intellectual problems and doctrinal
disputes with which Christianity has been concerned over
the relationship between the divine and the human in Jesus
Christ centre on the question: can there be visible, human
actions of which one may be certain that they have invisible
efects, i.e. perform an act of God? At all events, in some
cases (the forgiveness of sins, baptism, the Lord's Supper)
the Bible answers this question very clearly in the affirm-

ative. The number of these symbolic acts, called sacraments, was not fixed until the Middle Ages; before then, it ranged from two to thirty. It is the theology of the high Middle Ages which first mentions seven sacraments, a number which still holds today in the Roman and the Orthodox church. From the beginning there was never any dispute over the two most important sacraments, baptism and the eucharist/Lord's Supper – baptism as a sacrament of entry into the church and of the confession of Christ, the eucharist as the heart of Christian worship. The Reformation churches recognize only these two sacraments; for the Anglican church they are the major sacraments and the others are only minor sacraments. The latter, the five other sacraments of the Roman and Orthodox traditions, are in part rites relating to changes in life: confirmation as the reenactment of the outpouring of the Spirit at Pentecost and as a conscious assent at an adult age to infant baptism and initiation; marriage and ordination to the priesthood, understood as the basis of entry into a state and authority, for the order of sexuality on the one hand and for official service in the church on the other; the anointing of the sick as the sacrament of those whose life is in danger. The biblical promise of the forgiveness of sins underlies all the sacraments; it is summed up in the fifth minor sacrament, penance. This sacrament was resorted to in the early church only in connection with the gravest transgressions (apostasy from the faith, adultery, murder) and could not be repeated. Since the Middle Ages it has been developed into a regular means of pastoral care.

The Christian festivals distribute the most important events of the life, death and resurrection of Jesus over the course of the year, at points which partly correspond to the Jewish or pagan festivals. But the cycle of the church's year should not disguise the fact that Christianity is not a religion which thinks cyclically.

A drama with an exchange of roles

Judaism and Christianity have a common basis in the biblical view of history: the world has a beginning and an end; history is not ordered by the repetition of endless cycles, but progresses from the beginning of creation through the judgment at its end to the consummation which the Bible depicts in the image of the new or heavenly Jerusalem. God is a clear counterpart to the world: as creator God stands at the beginning, accompanies the drama of history, is its judge, and brings it to a happy ending. Similarly, the beginning and end of the individual's life lie outside human control in the hand of God, but that life must be lived responsibly, and to the end a reckoning will be required in the dramatic interplay of guilt and forgiveness.

The Christian belief that the last phase of history has already begun with the death and resurrection of Jesus of Nazareth on the one hand distinguishes Christianity from Judaism and on the other makes it more radical than Judaism: Christians live not only between creation and the last judgment but also between the beginning and the end of the end time, as it were with a sense of an even greater pace of history, of an even more urgent responsibility, since they are living near to the climax of the drama. There is no mistaking the fact that something of the unrest, dissatisfaction and impatience which have gone with Christianity from the beginning is also at work in the hectic character of the Western belief in progress.

The drama is played out in the interchange of light and shade, in the battle between good and evil. For all religions, suffering is a result of this opposition, and an unavoidable transitional pain. Interpretations range from punishment for wrongdoing to a test of one's trust in God (as in the Old Testament book of Job), and attempt to emphasize or play down the absurdity of human suffering by producing a logic of cause and effect; nevertheless, the question why God can allow the innocent to suffer has never been silenced.

Christianity has a completely new perspective on this question: those who believe in an incarnate God who has himself suffered have no need to explain suffering by one theory or another; it is more important to them that God is prepared for a saving exchange of roles and as a fellow-sufferer instigates reconciliation with the insoluble riddle of suffering. Christians need no longer understand suffering and death as a punishment or even as a test, but can interpret it as participation in the suffering of God himself, who is advancing the course of history to its eschatological destination through solidarity with those who suffer.

Whatever terrors human beings experience, nothing any longer excludes them from nearness to God. Accordingly, Christianity also announces an exchange of roles: solidarity with the suffering is the decisive criterion by which human beings are judged: those who help the suffering help God himself.

In the vision of the last judgment the judge and king asserts: '*I was hungry and you gave me food . . . I was a stranger and homeless and you took me in*', and to the question when and where this happened he replies:

'*I say to you, what you did to the least of my brothers you did to me.*'
      The Gospel according to Matthew, Chapter 24

We must keep this perspective in mind if we want to understand forms of piety and life in Christian history which often seem strange.

In prayers, worship, celebrations and customs the Christian relationship to God is often expressed in contradictory terms, paradoxically or in an exaggerated way because it denotes a God who is simultaneously omnipotent and helpless, impassible and suffering, eternal and dying, exalted and brotherly.

Christians are convinced that what human beings long for but cannot achieve of themselves, God himself undertakes, namely the reconciliation of eternity and finitude, heaven and earth.

Towards the third millennium?

One last question. Will the spiritual course of Christianity, which with all its twists and turns has led through two thousand years of history, also cross the threshold of the third millennium? Does this religion face entirely new challenges? Or are the old delusions and obstacles simply appearing in new guises?

The loss of relevance which the Christian churches have suffered over the last two centuries can be summed up in one word: secularization. The experience of mass defections from the churches and the decline of their influence in the public sphere, together with the emergence of ideologies hostile to religion and hopes of progress, might seem to have demonstrated conclusively that people would get on much better without religion. In response to this, theologians postulated a 'religionless Christianity' to prevent Christian faith being dragged down with the other religions: Christianity was said to have nothing in common with human religious gifts and needs. But in the meantime an opposite development has taken place: two world wars and the dire consequences of technological civilization have shattered belief in progress, while interest in religion in one form or another persists, even if less and less attention is paid to Christianity in its European heartlands.

> *So Paul, standing in the middle of the Areopagus, said: 'Men of Athens, I perceive that in every way you are very religious. For as I passed along, and observed the objects of your worship, I found also an altar with this inscription, "To an unknown God". What therefore you worship as unknown, this I proclaim to you.'*
>
> Acts 17

The new challenge to Christianity is the competition from the many forms of religion which seek to satisfy the human quest for salvation by borrowings and mixtures from every possible rite and cult, from elements of Eastern and archaic religions. A new Gnosticism promises spiritual transformations and an individual, esoteric way to a fulfilled life, of a kind that is no longer expected from Christianity. However, this situation is by no means new. From the beginning Christianity grew in the Hellenistic societies of the Roman empire, in which cults from many lands were practised and all kinds of philosophies, beliefs and superstitions were in vogue. Paul was not ashamed to make this diffuse and varied religiosity the starting point for his preaching: he presented the unknown God of pious pagans as the one God of Jews and Christians.

Throughout the history of Christianity, repeated reflection on its original intention has been the best prospect for its continuation. And that is also the case today. There will be no more Christian societies; the state will not protect Christianity any better than other religions. But whereas science will make the world less and less inexplicable, people will still have no control over trust and love, meeting and parting, sickness and death. God does not fill in the gaps still left by enlightened knowledge, but is the name for the one in whose hands Christians, with their belief in the incarnation, put the solution to the abiding riddle of life.

Much that the Christian churches have learned from the experience of 1500 years of social domination is now proving a hindrance to their credibility. What is being looked for is another approach more akin to Christian origins; fortunately, this approach has never disappeared completely from history and has produced saints and heretics, founders of religious orders and reformers to rescue Christianity and enable it to survive.

For this religion on the threshold of the third millennium, that could mean:

A return to the dynamics of its beginnings. The humanitarian aspects of Christianity can be presented more credibly without political power. Many religions have ethical principles, social commitment, and rites and festivals to mark the stages of life; however, the central message of the incarnate God makes Christianity unique. Concentration on this could set its initial dynamics in motion once again. Finally, Christianity has a long and fertile history of thought. The fundamentalist refusal to think can be seen as an understandable reaction to a Christianity which has forgotten itself and been dissipated in trivialities; but it also leads into a dead end, as does dissolving Christianity into a universal religion or reducing the churches to moral institutions.

Respect for humanity come of age. The churches do not need to be like political parties, standing up for party interests. It is their message which gives the churches credibility, and without the message the churches are superfluous. Where this is overlooked, the result is clericalism as the self-preservation of an officialdom. Institutions are unavoidable, but they will only be accepted if they keep up with the political sensibilities of the time and do not give their blessing to forms of life and government from past centuries. Thus a future Christianity will need to display the characteristics which marked this religion right from the start: believers who are personally convinced forming manageable communities instead of bureaucratic pastoral administration; ministry as a service which unites mature Christians instead of a centralistic body which allows them no initiatives; solidarity with fellow citizens in quest for a better society instead of a defence of traditional positions of political power. Presumably the offices and hierarchies which have developed in the churches in parallel to state administration will become less and less important for individual believers. That is especially true for the growing churches of the Third World, which will find it easier to distinguish between necessary order and its imported European form.

Communication instead of excommunication. The practice of the reciprocal exclusion of church groups and confessions has a long history, but from the nineteenth century onwards it has been increasingly recognized as a self-made obstacle to Christianity. In the ecumenical movement efforts have been made to replace excommunication with communication between different standpoints and traditions. This process can lead to tangible results if the plurality of Christian theologies and forms of organization are recognized and there is a desire for joint action. The progress made is unmistakable: after centuries of separation, over the past few decades it has become possible for the great Christian confessions – Catholics, Anglicans, Protestants and Orthodox – to pray together and work together. However, these convergences still seem inconsequential when one considers how far the churches still are from mutual recognition.

Witness instead of admonition. Obsessed with their former social significance, the Christian churches keep lapsing into complaint and accusation: past times are said to have been golden ages and contemporaries are blamed for the contraction of the churches. There is a kind of Christianity which feels insulted by the course of history and therefore is no longer in a position to carry conviction. But if Christianity is to have a history, it cannot demand complete belief in the doctrinal principles of two thousand years as a membership qualification. For Christianity cannot be reduced to the observance of rules of life and regulations for worship; it needs the personal history of each individual believer. Individual experiences, personal ideas, experiments in living. exploration of by-ways must be allowed, as long as the heart of Christianity is seriously kept in view: the conviction that there is a brotherly and sisterly God who has drawn near to humankind. Teaching and admonition can communicate this conviction only to a very limited degree: witness to it will be far more important.

'If you want to learn what Christian faith is,' says a text from the early church, 'come and spend a year in my house.'

Although Christianity is one of the three great monotheistic world religions, its image of God has many levels, with notable consequences for the everyday life of believers.

As a spiritual way this religion preserves something of the endtime expectation of its early days, in the awareness

that the drama of one's own life is caught up in the drama of salvation history,

that we are striving for a clear goal,

and that until it is reached the world is to be shaped with utter dedication, without compelling paradise,

and that in the unavoidable suffering of the meantime we have a brotherly and sisterly God at our side.

For further reading

Here are just a few books which may help towards a deeper understanding:

1. The Bible and guides to reading

Of the many modern translations of the Bible, the Revised Standard Version, the Jerusalem Bible, the Revised English Bible and the New International Version will be found particularly helpful.

For commentary and further helps to study see the two volumes by Étienne Charpentier, *How to Read the Old Testament* and *How to Read the New Testament*, SCM Press and Crossroad Publishing Company 1982. For Jesus see Gerd Theissen, *The Shadow of the Galilean*, SCM Press and Fortress Press 1987, and for Paul E. P. Sanders, *Paul*, Oxford University Press 1991.

2. Church history and doctrine

For more detail on church history see the two volumes by Jean Comby, *How to Read Church History*, SCM Press and Crossroad Publishing Company 1985, 1988: the first goes up to the Reformation, the second to the present day; also Diarmaid MacCulloch, *Groundwork of Christian History*, Epworth Press 1986. Hans Küng, *Credo*, SCM Press and Doubleday 1993, provides an attractive introduction to doctrine; see also his *Great Christian Thinkers*, SCM Press and Continuum Publishing Group 1994.

3. Reference

The Oxford Dictionary of the Christian Church ed. F. L. Cross and E. A. Livingstone, second edition, Oxford University Press 1974, is an unrivalled source of information (a third edition will appear shortly); for details of the many intellectual figures in Christian history see John Bowden, *Who's Who in Theology*, SCM Press and Crossroad Publishing Company 1990.